A LIFELONG LOVE AFFAIR

A Lifelong
LOVE AFFAIR

Keeping Sexual Desire Alive
in Your Relationship

JOSEPH NOWINSKI

THORSONS PUBLISHING GROUP

First UK Edition 1989

First published by Dodd, Mead & Company, Inc.,

71 Fifth Avenue, New York, NY 10003

© Joseph Nowinski 1988

Author's Note
Although the substance of this book is based on clinical experience, the case material has been extensively altered to protect the confidentiality and identity of the individuals. The use of dialogue is a literary device and does not reflect verbatim clinical material.

British Library Cataloguing in Publication Data

Nowinski, Joseph
A lifelong love affair: keeping sexual desire alive in your relationship.
1. Sex relations. Psychological aspects
I. Title
155.3'4

ISBN 0-7225-1792-0

Printed in Great Britain by Biddles Limited, Guildford Surrey

Published by Thorsons Publishing Group, Wellingborough,
Northamptonshire NN8 2RQ, England.

1 3 5 7 9 10 8 6 4 2

For my parents
Helen and Joe Nowinski

Contents

INTRODUCTION   ix

I

Falling Out of Love:
Problems of Intimacy and
Sexual Desire   1

1 After the Revolution: Sex, Intimacy, and Love   3
2 People Without Passion   21
3 Intimate Relationships   39
4 I'm Too Old for That, and Other Myths About
Intimacy and Passion   53

II

Working on Love   69

5 Working Alone   71
6 Working Together   93

III

Getting in Touch   117

7 Sexual Fantasy   119
8 Body Images   143

CONTENTS

IV

The Heart of Love 163

9 Self-Esteem 165

10 Trust 191

V

*Liberating
Passion and Intimacy* 213

11 Egalitarian Marriage 215

INDEX 241

Introduction

This book is about staying in love. It's a book about intimacy and sexual passion. It's *not* a book for people who are trying to decide *if* they want a relationship, or *if* they want to make a commitment. This is a book for people who *have* a relationship that they want to keep. This relationship may not be perfect, but it's based on a real commitment, which includes a commitment to work on it if that's what it takes to make things better.

This is also a book for people who don't want to settle for just any kind of relationship. It's a book for people who believe in commitment, but who also believe that commitment without fulfillment is not enough to sustain a relationship. In their hearts these people believe in love: in the possibility of having commitment *and* intimacy *and* passion.

Good relationships are intimate and passionate relationships. They are built on a foundation of involvement, of sharing, and of sexual desire that doesn't fade with time. Couples who stay in love describe each other as friends and lovers. If anything, the feelings of connectedness that bind them together grow stronger, not weaker, over time. They can talk to each other better than they can talk to anyone else. They can laugh with each other, and be playful with each other. If you talk with them—or just sit back and watch them—you can't help being impressed by how their relationship hasn't lost its spark. They'll tell you that time changes love, but that the love is still very much alive. These couples stay interested in each other. They can open themselves to each other, and the trust between them is strong enough that they can be vulnerable with each other.

Couples who stay in love also maintain their sexual interest in each other. Sex, too, may change with time, but contrary to the cliché about sexual desire ending with the honeymoon, these couples have achieved a level of sexual relating that honeymooners can only envy. They often say that sex has improved over time.

This book assumes that the breakdown of a relationship that was once good always begins with a breakdown of intimacy. Intimacy is the bedrock of successful and fulfilling relationships. When intimacy fades, love fades. When intimacy is eroded, sexual passion can't last, either. And, under those conditions, eventually even the strongest commitment may fail.

What causes breakdowns of intimacy and problems of sexual desire? To put it differently, why do people fall *out of* love? Is it immaturity? Neurosis? Weak character? Is there something profoundly wrong with people whose relationships are less than they would like them to be?

In the past, problems of intimacy and sexual desire were typically considered to be problems of *individuals*. Women who were turned off to sex were said to be suffering from "blocks" or "hangups." They were called "frigid." Women who felt alienated from or angry at their husbands were seen as castrating. The problem, we thought, was caused by something within them as individuals. The same thinking applied to men. After all, we reasoned, aren't all men *naturally* interested in sex?

This book departs from such naive thinking and outdated views. Instead, it assumes that the principal causes of low sexual desire and alienation are to be found in our *relationships;* in other words, in the way we relate to each other. It is based on these simple ideas: that nothing turns a woman (or a man) on better than being treated as an equal; and that nothing facilitates wanting to get close to another person more than feeling that we're on an equal footing with that person.

Problems of sexual desire, like problems of intimacy, can be accounted for by things (like distrust, powerlessness, and low self-esteem) that create *inequality* between lovers. Overcoming those barriers, and building the kind of relationship that can sustain sexual passion and intimacy for a lifetime, is what this book is about.

Today we stand on the verge of an era of new potential for relationships. There is renewed interest in commitment and monogamy. But that's not to say that people want a return to the past. The sexual revolution won't be reversed. It's changed forever the ways that men and women see themselves, and the expectations they have for themselves and their relationships. It's created new possibilities. At the same time, the truth is that men and women today are anxious and insecure about the prospects for commitment and monogamy. They're uncertain about how to turn potentials into realities.

This book will be helpful to people who have (or can find) a little faith, who have not become so cynical about love and commitment that they've given up on relationships. If you still believe in love, if your heart is open and alive, and if you believe that it's possible to stay in love with one person for the rest of your life, then this book may be very helpful to you.

PART I

Falling Out of Love: Problems of Intimacy and Sexual Desire

Who has problems of sexual desire and intimacy? What are the causes of these problems? More importantly, what can couples do in order to rekindle intimacy and passion that may have faded, or to keep them from slipping away?

To begin answering questions like these, we need to take a closer look at problems of intimacy and sexual desire. Our goal is to understand better how couples fall out of love. Then, using that understanding, we'll start talking about what you can do about it, and how you can prevent it. ❧

1

After the Revolution: Sex, Intimacy, and Love

The sexual revolution is over. In place of the uproar, the experimentation, the hopeful promise, the sheer fun and excitement of the sixties and seventies, is an atmosphere of anxiety and insecurity that borders at times on paranoia. In the span of a few years, we've gone from being playful and willing to being fearful and serious about sex. Instead of being open to risks in relationships, we've become cautious. Unlike the intense, clamorous calls for change that were the hallmarks of a decade ago, the news today is dominated by fearsome headlines marking the slow but steady progress of insidious and sometimes fatal diseases. Revolution has been replaced by reactionism, openness by conservatism, and excitement by anxiety. Warnings about the dire consequences of unguarded sexuality and experimentation abound. Magazines that once featured articles on open marriage and overcoming sexual inhibitions now talk of sexual abstinence. Fear is afoot in our society, and it is spreading quickly. It promises to affect our attitudes and behaviour profoundly; in what ways, and to what extent, we still don't know.

❦　　❦　　❦

Though the sexual revolution is over, the news isn't all bad. Though we live in an age of anxiety, there still are possibilities and potentials to be fulfilled. People today are intensely interested in commitment again, and in monogamy. They want to find the right partner and make a relationship work. Sure, they have their doubts, lots of them, and a lot of fears. They aren't sure that relationships can really last a lifetime and still be good. On some level they've lost faith. They worry that commitment is a trap, and in their more cynical moments they wonder whether monogamy isn't just another fairy tale.

You might conclude that all this renewed interest in commitment and monogamy means that people want to undo all of the changes that came from the sexual revolution. You might take it as evidence that the revolution was a mistake at best, or downright evil at worst. You might think this, but you'd be wrong. The people I talk to do want relationships. They are more willing today to think in terms of personal sacrifice and commitment, as well as personal growth and freedom. But the lessons of the sexual revolution and the liberation movement are real and lasting. We want commitment, but we don't want commitment without love, monogamy without passion, or sacrifice without fulfillment. What we want is to be able to integrate intimacy and passion with a commitment and monogamy. That might seem like a tall order, and maybe it is. But that's what couples today are aiming for.

Some of the first people who noticed the changes in our society were the sex therapists, whose practices had thrived during the decade of the sexual revolution. The first signs of change came when a new breed of client began appearing in their offices, asking for help with problems that they weren't used to handling. Instead of being asked to help overcome problems of sexual performance, like impotence or anorgasmia, therapists suddenly found themselves being asked to help with something that was entirely different, and that they weren't at all prepared for.

Who were these new clients? What were their new and different problems? Basically, they were people who did *not* have any trouble performing in bed. In a word, they were sexually functional. The men had little or no trouble getting erections, or controlling ejaculation. The women were orgasmic. They had all read all the popular books about sexual enhancement, and they all knew just about as much about the how-to's of making love as the therapists themselves. Sexual inhibitions and poor technique were not their problem.

So what was the problem? The problem was that although these people were sexually functional, even skilful at making love, they were sexually frustrated and unhappy, not because they couldn't perform, or because they were inhibited or lacking in technique, but because sex didn't make them feel the way they wanted to, about themselves or about each other. Many of them had lost or were losing their interest in sex, and most of them were experiencing alienation instead of the intimacy they were looking for in their relationships. Some had to be dragged into therapy by angry partners under threat of divorce. Most, though, came willingly, frustrated in their relationships, and feeling that something was missing.

As important as the fact that these new clients wanted help with different kinds of issues, was the fact that they did *not* want to end their relationships as a way of dealing with their unhappiness and frustrations. They were not interested in divorce. They held no illusions that simply changing partners would be the answer. They did not want open marriages, either. They were not interested in learning about any new sexual techniques. Of course they wanted good sex. But most of all they wanted their relationships to work on the level of passionate involvement and intimacy.

What the sex therapists eventually realized was that, with their new clients, they weren't dealing with sex at all; instead, they were dealing with love. Problems of sexual desire and intimacy have grown to become not only the most difficult, but also the most common problems confronting sex therapists and marriage counselors throughout America today. Armed with their knowledge of behavioural sex-therapy programmes like those pioneered by Masters and Johnson, therapists have tried their best to help. It has been frustrating work. In stark contrast to the enormous success they had grown accustomed to, they have found these cases complicated and difficult. But then again, what else could you expect when you're dealing with an issue no less complicated and involved than that of staying in love?

Problems of sexual desire have a lot to do with problems of intimacy. It's rare that you find one without the other. In turn, you could say that sexual passion and intimacy together have a lot to do with what we call *love*. They are, really, the basic ingredients of love, the foundation of a lasting and fulfilling relationship.

We know now that problems of intimacy and sexual desire are more than the burden of an unfortunate few. Who are these people. Are they ill, or mentally disturbed? Are they missing something, physically or psychologically, compared to everyone else? Do they come from broken homes? Are their problems a reflection of some grave personal inadequacy? Are they all neurotics? *No.* They are men like Dave: thirty-seven years old, a successful lawyer, a loving husband and father of two. They are women like Fran: thirty years old, college educated, full-time mother and part-time teacher, an avid jogger and an accomplished artist.

People with problems of intimacy and sexual desire—who are struggling on a day-to-day basis with the issue of staying together and staying in love—come from every walk of life, from every kind of background. They are rich, middle-class, and poor; they are young, middle-aged, and older. They are often married, but sometimes they're living together. They are very often educated and successful. They are anything but odd, weird, sick, or disturbed. Look around you. They are your friends and neighbours, your colleagues and co-workers. They include your relatives. They are, in a very real sense, the heart and soul of our society.

Sex and Love

What exactly is it that people are looking to get out of sex? That's a question I'm asked a lot. Sometimes it's an angry, frustrated person who's doing the asking. It's a fair question, though, and one that we've probably all asked ourselves at one time or another.

Take a few minutes, grab a pencil and paper, and write down all the different reasons you can think of that people have sex. After you've done that, check off the three reasons for having sex that are most important to *you*.

Whenever I've asked an audience to do this short exercise, the first thing I'm usually struck by is how many different reasons people can think of for having sex. Among the most frequent responses are things such as *fun, release, communicating love, being intimate,* and *pleasure*. People usually also think of some reasons for having sex that aren't necessarily so positive, like *dominance, aggression,* or *control*.

The fact that we can use sex for so many different purposes leads us to overburden our sexual relationships. We use sex for so many different purposes—to satisfy so many different needs—that sometimes we can't help being disappointed or frustrated. Men in particular are inclined to equate sex with intimacy, instead of seeing it as one *way* to be intimate. But women, too, are often guilty of expecting their sexual relationships to be all things to them: to be a means of expressing love, of getting close and being affectionate, to meet needs for pleasure and release, and to be just plain fun. Sometimes we even look to sex as a way to vent our anger, to quell our insecurities, to make peace, or to get something we want.

By expecting so much from sex, we often stand in our own

way, making it difficult for sex to do any one thing well for us. Couples set themselves up for conflict when partners try to use sex for incompatible purposes: when one is looking for intimacy, gentle affection, and love, while the other wants intensity and release. When I see a couple trying to satisfy too many needs at one time through sex, or using sex for very different reasons, I also find conflict and frustration.

Another thing I notice when I ask a group of people to list their reasons for having sex is how long it usually takes before someone says something about making babies. We share a good laugh at that, but the serious message beneath the laughter is that people today are almost exclusively interested in what sex can do for them *emotionally*. Then again, maybe they've always been that way. Maybe making babies has always been pretty low on the list of reasons for having sex.

Whether it's big news or old hat, the fact is that people are interested in sex mainly for its power to make them feel good and to feel close to each other. When they sense that sex is not doing those things for them, people start feeling unhappy.

Sex can have a lot to do with love or nothing at all to do with love. Sex and love can be completely independent or intimately connected. For one person, sex may always (and only) be a way to express intimate love. For someone else it may be the only way of being affectionate. A person may use sex strictly as a means of influencing others, usually because they feel powerless otherwise; another may look to it for relaxation. To complicate matters further, many people seem to use sex for different purposes at different times, and most try to use it for several different purposes at once.

So, if you're looking to find the answer to what sex has to do with love, or why people make love, you might as well realize that the answer is not simple. All that really matters is what sex means to you, how it fits into your relationship, and what you and your partner use it for. Are your motivations compatible, and if not, why? When are you looking for the same things from sex, and when are you not? How else, besides sex, can you satisfy some of your needs?

Books and Covers

As you may already have guessed, the answer to why a person would lose interest in sex, why a person might find it difficult to be intimate, and why couples fall out of love, can be pretty complicated. One thing I've learned as a therapist is the truth in certain adages, like not judging a book by its cover, or not judging someone else until you've walked in their shoes. In dealing with relationships, things are not always as simple as they may seem, and a hasty therapist can do more harm than good.

Take, for example, the following case:

Jane and Jack had been married only six months, and after talking to them for an hour I found myself wondering whether they'd make it through another six. She was thirty-five; he was forty. She was divorced, a single parent with a young child; he'd never been married. Life for her had more or less been one long uphill battle, a story of self-denial and living pretty much from hand to mouth. Jack, on the other hand, had always been successful. He was used to having more money than he really needed, and his lifestyle had been nothing if not comfortable. But he'd been intensely attracted to Jane, pursued her and got involved, and finally found himself thinking of marriage.

From the moment I laid eyes on him, I could see that Jack was an angry man. He sat in his chair scowling. His greeting as we shook hands was little more than a grunt, uttered in a voice that was hard and flat. He sat down and folded his arms. I found myself feeling edgy.

I soon learned that it was Jack who was responsible for them being there. He'd insisted on it, he said. In his firm, hard voice, he explained rather matter-of-factly that the reason they were there was to get Jane's sexual problem "fixed." I got the impression that he meant business—that whatever the problem was, he wanted it fixed, and *now*. I took a deep breath. "What exactly *is* the problem?" I asked.

Jack glanced at Jane. Other than a short introductory hello, she had said nothing at all so far. Like Jack, though, and despite her silence, she gave me the impression that she was simmering with anger. I decided not to trifle with it for the time being.

Jack spoke again. Beneath the hardness, I could detect more than a touch of bitterness and sarcasm in his voice. "My wife," he explained, "seems to have become sexually frigid after marrying me. Since the *day* she married me, in fact"—he scowled at Jane—"she's been pretty much a cold fish."

I looked at Jane. Hard words, I thought. I waited for her response. But she just sat there. She didn't say a thing. The expression on her face was impassive. She calmly returned my gaze, and made no move to defend herself. I was puzzled by her apparent coolness, and a little unnerved by it.

Jack continued. He described in detail how Jane had rejected his sexual advances, beginning on their wedding night. "But not before then," he added. The implication was clear: He was suggesting that he'd been manipulated into the marriage, only to be dropped just as soon as Jane had got what she was after.

Jack's story sounded plausible, especially since I still hadn't heard Jane's side. After all, he wouldn't have been the first man in history to be lured into a marriage of convenience, or security. Also, Jane's strange silence bothered me. I couldn't understand how she could just sit there and not react to what was being said. I was expecting a defence, and the lack of it threw my sympathies toward Jack.

It wasn't until very close to the end of that first hour that Jane finally sat up in her chair. I watched her slow, deliberate movements. Suddenly I realized that she was going to speak, and I felt my pulse quicken.

As Jane spoke, Jack looked away. But that didn't deter her at all. Once she started, she spoke her mind. It was true, she said, that she'd started feeling turned off to Jack, and it was true, too, that it had started as soon as they were married. "Yes," she said, looking at his turned head, daring him with her eyes to return her angry stare, "it *was* on our wedding night that it started." Then she turned to me. "I've never been so fooled in my life," she said. "I thought he wanted a relationship, a marriage, but all he wanted was sex, a body to screw twice a week. Tell me," she said, her eyes burning into Jack again, "isn't it true that if I just let you have sex twice a week, you'd be perfectly happy? We wouldn't be here at all, isn't that right?"

I looked at Jack. There was a tense moment before he responded. "Yes," he said, speaking to me instead of Jane, "I suppose that's right. Other than for the sex, she's been a good wife."

"What does that mean?" I asked.

"It means," he explained, "that she takes good care of the house. She cooks, she cleans. Things like that. She's a good housekeeper. But as a sex partner she stinks."

I turned to Jane. "And what about you?" I asked. "If Jack's complaint is sex, what's yours? Do you have any?"

Jane had quite a long list of complaints, starting with the fact that as far as she was concerned it was Jack, not her, who had changed just as soon they were married. The ways he had changed, she said, were the reasons she got turned off to sex.

I asked Jane to tell me about the changes in Jack. There were a lot of them, she said, but basically they all boiled down to the fact that he'd stopped putting any effort into the relationship once they were married. During their year-long courtship, she explained, he'd been attentive, caring, and considerate. He took care of how he looked. Whenever he saw her, he was dressed neatly. The man she'd wanted to marry, she explained, had been an attractive man, who liked having fun. He was someone who seemed interested in her, to whom she could talk for hours on end.

"But all that stopped," she said, "just as soon as he knew he had me. Then he got lazy, like he is today. Now all he wants to do is watch television every night. When he wants sex, he won't even bother to brush his teeth or see to it that he's clean. He expects me to drop whatever I'm doing and hop into bed with him whenever *he's* ready. I'm sorry, but I don't work that way."

Well, I thought, that added an interesting wrinkle to the story! Which version, I wondered, was right? It was like one of those mystery stories where the clues change depending on who's un-covering them. To get to the bottom of it, I knew I needed a lot more information.

Things started getting clearer as I began to fill in the picture, over several sessions, of the story of Jack and Jane's relationship. To some extent, I learned, they both were right: Jane did start rejecting Jack, but only after he stopped courting her. That happened mainly after they were married, though there had been warning signs before then. Jane chose not to heed those warning signs, a decision she later regretted. She had tried to be patient and understanding. Instead of speaking up, she had kept quiet about little things that bothered her. She'd been quiet about big things, too, like the fact that Jack seemed to want his lifestyle to stay exactly the way it had been before he was married. So, they ended up sleeping in the bed that he'd shared with many other women, instead of getting the new one that Jane wanted. They kept the furniture he liked, the paintings he liked, and put her things in the basement. All of them. Jane went along with this.

Within a month of getting married, Jane was having second thoughts. She was beginning to feel used. She was getting bitter quickly. But still she kept her feelings to herself. She convinced herself that Jack had been acting for that whole year of court-ship. Her trust in him quickly eroded, and with it went much of the closeness and passion she'd felt. From that very first night, when they made love in Jack's old bed, she sensed that he wasn't feeling the same emotions that she was, that he wasn't looking for the same things that she was from marriage. But she never confronted him. Instead, beginning at that moment she started to fall out of love with him.

Low sexual desire and alienation are not diseases, but forms of human *malaise*. The difference is that a disease has a physical cause, and may have a medical cure. The causes of malaise, on the other hand, lie in our hearts and minds, and the cures are to be found in the way we relate to ourselves and others. The reasons why people fall out of love have to do with the way they structure their relationships, the way they feel about themselves and their values.

There is no single "type" of person who loses interest in sex, or one reason why some couples lose the intimacy they once knew. Each relationship is unique, and every person's story is their own. The couples I work with come from all sorts of backgrounds. They have all kinds of personalities, and in many ways the causes (and cures) for their troubles are unique to each of them. This book, therefore, doesn't aim to stereotype people who fall out of love. We can't just lump all these people and relationships together and prescribe the same exact treatment. There is no neat "programme" for restoring intimacy and passion to a relationship. But there are things you can do. Your task will be to understand your own relationship, your own psyche, and to follow the path that fits you best. This book offers a sets of tools that you can use. What you create with these tools is very much up to you.

Changing Relationships

Change begins with understanding. Once you've gained some understanding of where you've come from, and what some of the causes might be for whatever problems and frustrations you're experiencing, you're in a position to do something about them. Understanding, though, is not the same as change. It's only half the process of growth and development. In addition to understanding—or "insight"—there needs to be *action*.

Action is what you need to add to insight in order to make things better. To be perfectly blunt, knowing what's wrong won't do you much good if you aren't prepared to *do* something about it. Therapies—or books—that stop at the level of insight aren't good enough. That's why this book has *two* goals: understanding and action. It tries not to leave you off at the point where you've gained some insights into why you are where you are. It aims to give you some practical guidelines for action.

To help facilitate change, this book will present you with many different methods and techniques that people I've worked with have found helpful. In many cases they have been instrumental in devising and refining these techniques. Not every one of them will be useful to you, any more than all the insights presented here will fit you. It will be up to you to sort through the insights and guidelines for change, to see which ones fit you best, and decide what directions you want to go in.

Another thing I've learned as a therapist is that action can be a lot harder than insight. It can be much easier to sit back and say, "Aha, I see!" than it is to do something about what you see. At times when I've found myself faced with this uncomfortable situation, of seeing the light but feeling afraid to change, I take comfort in the knowledge that it isn't any easier for anyone else. We are all excited by and, at the same time, afraid of the unknown. It is much easier to cling to old ways and familiar surroundings than it is to strike out anew. And building a fulfilling relationship—staying in love—is very much like that. It's a journey, in some ways, into the unknown. So, expect yourself to be afraid at times, as well as excited. And have courage. You're not alone.

Holding Back: Fears of Intimacy and Passion

"I guess you could say I'm pretty disgusted," said Ellie. Her tone of voice matched the look on her face. Then it changed, became sad, and I saw tears well in her eyes. She sighed.

Ellie's husband John, meanwhile, sat across the room from her and sheepishly avoided looking in her direction. Though it seemed obvious to me that he was feeling bad, he wasn't saying much. I wondered what he was feeling and thinking.

The situation was a familiar one to me. John struck me as a man who was holding back, bottling up his thoughts and feelings instead of letting them out. That's a pretty common trait of men and women who have trouble expressing sexual passion or being intimate in relationships.

Why was John holding back? That was the question that Ellie needed an answer to. Beyond that, she needed to know what she—or better yet, *they*—could do to change things. These are questions that many others need answers to, also. They wonder, is it me? Am I sexually undesirable? Am I boring? Is that why my partner seems turned off and disinterested? Is there something about me that makes it difficult for others to get close or open up to me?

In John's case, the roots of the problem ran deep. Holding back had started in his childhood. It was a pattern that had been with him for so long it seemed like part of his nature, like the colour of his eyes, like the shape of his hands. It had caused him plenty of trouble, too, ruining one marriage and now threatening another. Both of his wives had felt that John held back. He wouldn't say what he was feeling, or what was on his mind. He wouldn't argue, wouldn't ask for things, wouldn't pursue them for sex. Both had felt shut out and rejected, and ultimately very angry. And now that it was happening for the second time, John had to admit that there might be something to what they were saying.

I figured that the reasons why John had closed off, and why he'd always had a hard time opening up in a relationship, lay in the way his family had related to him while he was growing up. Learning the specifics about these things, though, wasn't easy. People like John aren't exactly open books. You get a sense that they're feeling something, thinking something, but it can be damn difficult to get them to tell you what it is. They don't like to reveal much of themselves, either emotions or thoughts, or their personal histories, for that matter. They prefer to keep everything to themselves concerning where they've come from and what it was like there. Usually, if you ask them what they're thinking, or what they're feeling, they'll shrug and say "nothing." We can all respect a person's privacy, but these people are being more than private. In many ways the doors to their hearts and minds are locked and guarded, not for the sake of privacy, but out of fear and distrust.

The truth is that probably the only reason John did begin opening up was fear. He believed he'd be divorced again if he didn't open up. Despite his trouble opening up to his wife, he really did love her and didn't want to lose her. He relied on her love, and he wanted her to stay with him. In her heart Ellie knew what she meant to him; but that knowledge itself wasn't enough to sustain her. She needed more than faith, more than an occasional word. She needed to get back some of the love and caring she'd been giving to John for the past ten years. Neither intimacy nor sexual passion can be one-way streets if you expect them to last.

"I suppose you could say I've always been this way," said John. He was talking about his lack of emotion, about the way he held back his thoughts and feelings. "I know I have trouble showing Ellie I love her. I know I tend to keep things to myself. Sometimes I wish she'd just take my word for it that I love her, and leave it at that. But I guess you're right. That isn't enough. Maybe it wouldn't be enough for any woman.

"As far back as I can remember, I've more or less lived in my own little world. I can remember being that way as a kid. I had four older brothers and a father. That's it. No sisters, no mother. I suppose you could say that I was at the bottom of the totem pole. *Way* at the bottom. In my house nobody listened to me. And I mean *nobody*. No one cared what I felt, what I thought. I don't mean it to make it sound like I'm feeling sorry for myself, but the truth is I don't think anybody hardly knew that I existed, much less cared about me one way or another. Until I met my first wife. She was the first person I'd ever met who made me feel like I mattered to somebody."

How would that kind of an upbringing make *you* feel? Do you imagine that being raised in that kind of environment would lead you to being an open person? Is it the kind of childhood you'd want to talk about, or want to forget?

John grew up to be a man who in some ways was tough and

independent—that was the outside. On the inside, though, it was a different story. Underneath the thick skin was a delicate, almost fragile centre. He was a painfully shy, very insecure man whose opinion of himself pretty well matched his image of the bottom of the totem pole. He didn't believe he was worth much, so he rarely tried hard to get what he wanted. In his heart he'd grown up feeling powerless. Holding back, as you'll learn, is the common denominator among people who feel powerless.

In relationships John avoided even the slightest confrontation. Rather than fight, he'd sooner give in. He couldn't understand why that would even bother someone else, much less how it could drive a person crazy. He was baffled over why both his first wife, and now Ellie, had ended up being so angry at him. I could understand it, though. As Ellie put it, "I'd like to see some spunk in John. I'd like to see some feeling in him. Just once I'd like to see him get angry at me for something. I tell you, I'd actually be grateful to hear him disagree with me once in a while! But the way he is, it's like being married to a zombie. I swear, if I didn't talk, there'd never be a word said between us. If I stopped coming on to him for sex, we'd have no sex life, either."

When she first met him, Ellie actually liked John's quiet nature. She'd been in just the opposite kind of relationship before, and in many ways John was refreshing. He wasn't demanding. He was considerate and gentle. She realized that he was very quiet and shy, but she figured that would change in time. It didn't.

All the while they were dating, and even for the first year or so of their marriage, Ellie didn't mind so much being the one who initiated sex. John seemed to enjoy it well enough, and again she told herself that being the one to take the lead was a lot better than being pushed around or forced into sex, which had happened to her at one time.

Around the time of their second anniversary, Ellie started realizing how little John had changed. It started bothering her that he never initiated lovemaking. It also started to bother her that he always went along with what she wanted, and agreed with whatever she said, even when she suspected that he wanted something else or had a different opinion from hers. She asked him once or twice about sex—about whether there was anything he especially liked when it came to making love—but he just shrugged and said that what they did was just fine with him. She dropped the subject and tried to forget it, but eventually it got to her. His habit of always going along with whatever she wanted irritated her. She found herself starting to pick fights. She knew it was a mean and spiteful thing to do, but she couldn't help herself. "I just had to see what would happen," she said, "whether I could get a rise out of him." But nothing happened. John didn't fight back, and that stirred Ellie up even more.

Ellie eventually put the sex issue to the test. She held out to see if John would come on to her. He didn't. She got mad. She yelled, then felt guilty. He'd apologize, and then he'd initiate sex—once—and the cycle would start over. When they came to see me they'd been caught up in this pattern for about two years, and in all that time had made love only two or three times.

Karen and Mark were another typical case of a couple that was falling out of love. Again, their problems mainly had to do with intimacy and sexual desire. Despite the fact that in many ways they'd had a solid marriage for five years, they were now on the verge of divorce. Karen, in particular, was so angry that I wasn't sure at first if I'd be able to help them at all.

According to Karen, the trouble with Mark was that he was oversexed. From her perspective, he was very much the macho type. But from where I sat, Mark seemed just the opposite. I thought he seemed rather sensitive; in fact, if anything, I'd have described him as unaggressive. His approach to Karen was always mild and gentle, his attitude considerate in the extreme. In other words, the impression I got was just the opposite of what I associate with the word "macho."

As time went on, my initial impressions of Mark's personality were reinforced. I watched him give in, time and time again, when in his shoes I thought I'd have fought a little harder, pushed for my point of view, or tried to get what I wanted. I saw him avoid even minor confrontations. He seemed willing to take the blame for all the trouble between him and Karen, though doing so never gave him the peace I suspected he hoped to buy.

By avoiding issues and keeping his feelings to himself, Mark was holding back in his relationship with Karen, and in his case, too, the pattern had its roots in feelings of powerlessness. He'd been raised by domineering parents whose main concern always seemed to be with impressions more than with substance, with being successful more than with being happy. Under these circumstances, Mark never developed a strong sense of himself, or much faith in his ability to set his own course or get what he wanted in life. This attitude was slowly killing his marriage. He'd been withdrawn from Karen for years, and though he didn't fight with her, he didn't communicate with her, either. The alienation that she felt, combined with his apparent lack of interest in making love, was driving her crazy. Karen was actually wrong about Mark being a macho man, but his unwillingness to come out from his shell made it impossible to confront that issue.

One thing that people like John and Mark have in common with others who hold back is their distrust and their deep sense of powerlessness. They may not recognize their distrust for what it is, or consciously realize that they feel powerless, but their inability to trust others, their avoidance of confrontation and conflict, keep them from opening up in relationships. Their partners feel shut out, frustrated, and angry. The irony is that they often create their own self-fulfilling prophecies: by starving the very relationships that could nourish them, they reinforce their own alienation. They drive people away, or let them slip away, and then feel rejected.

The most important lesson to be gained from these two brief sketches is that one of the most important differences between people who are in touch with their passion, and who can be intimate, versus those who can't, has to do with holding back.

Everyone possesses the potential to experience intense sexual passion. *Everyone* has the potential to feel intensely intimate and connected with someone they love. It isn't a matter of there being something missing in those 20 to 40 percent of couples who are frustrated for lack of intimacy or sexual passion. The challenge is to liberate the potentials that are already there in each and every one of them.

2

People Without Passion

It isn't easy to characterize people who have problems of sexual desire, or to characterize relationships that lack intimacy. As a group, individuals and couples with these problems don't fit into any single mould. Experience has taught me that what may be very true in one case may not apply at all in another. Still, certain issues or themes do come up often enough to be able to draw some conclusions about the conditions that make lasting intimacy and passion a possibility. Without these conditions, it's unlikely that a man or woman will be very sexual, or that a relationship will be very intimate. On the other hand, the more the conditions are met, the better the chances are for both to happen. In this chapter, we'll examine some of the commonalities among people who lose their sexual desire. In this chapter, we'll look more closely at problems of intimacy.

Powerlessness and Low Sexual Desire

A sense of powerlessness, which at times may even be unconscious, almost invariably underlies problems of sexual desire. This sense of powerlessness—of being one-down—is almost always present to some degree or another in people who lack or lose their interest in sex. More than any of the other subjects of this chapter, powerlessness is something that links these people as a group.

People who lack power respond to their situation in one of two ways: either they *lose* their sexuality, or else they try to *use* their sexuality to manipulate others. Holding back, and especially holding back sexually, is often the last refuge of a man or woman who feels powerless and frustrated in his/her relationship. Let me give you an example.

Laura and John had been married for eight years and had two young children. They came to see me because John was threatening a divorce unless Laura got over her sexual "hangups." Translated, that meant that Laura had lost most of her interest in sex. To add to John's feelings of rejection and anger, I learned from them that Laura had had a brief affair that ended when John found out about it. At first he'd wanted a divorce. But Laura pleaded with him. She said she wanted their marriage to work. She was willing, she said, to go to a therapist to try to work on "her" problem. That's where I came in.

As we filled in the picture of John and Laura's marriage, a pattern emerged that I've since become very familiar with. The first element in the pattern is low self-esteem. Laura, it seemed, had some significant problems in this area. She was a very attractive woman, but she was filled with anxieties and doubts not only about that, but about mostly everything else about herself. She was bright and artistically talented, but she hesitated to pursue her potentials for lack of confidence. She also had doubts about her adequacy as a mother and fretted over all the "mistakes" she made with her children, the kind of normal mistakes that all parents make every day.

John's personality was almost the opposite of Laura's. Whereas she was filled with self-doubt, on the surface at least he was all self-confidence. He was a self-made man who'd taken life by the horns and made it work for him. She worried all the time about others; he worried about himself. While Laura found it hard to make even minor decisions, John found it easy to make decisions not only for himself, but for her as well. As a result, John was very much in the driver's seat in the marriage. He had very definite ideas of what he expected from a wife and mother, and he pushed for what he wanted.

Laura, in contrast, didn't push at all. In response to my asking about fights, she smiled shyly and said, "John and I don't really fight."

"So," I said, "what do you do when you get angry?"

"I *don't* get angry," replied Laura. She seemed surprised that I would even suggest such an idea. "John gets angry. I get *upset.*"

"Oh," I said. "So, tell me what happens when you get upset."

"I just get quiet. That's one of our problems—we can go for days without speaking to each other. I think it's because I'd sooner avoid a fight than deal with it. I hate fighting."

"Why do you hate fighting?" I asked.

"Because I can't really defend myself," Laura replied.

"What do you mean?"

"I mean it's hard for me to find the right words. John's so much better than I am with words. Whenever I try to stand up for myself, I end up feeling like I'm wrong. It makes me think I'm really screwed up."

"Do you think," I asked, "that you might tend to *start out* an argument feeling that you're wrong?"

"Yes. I've never thought of it that way, but now that you mention it, I do feel that way. Like I'm wrong from the beginning."

"When did you start feeling that way?"

"I've *always* felt that way. Ever since I was a kid. My father was a very critical man, and I never felt that I could argue with him. My mother, too, for that matter. They'd always make me feel wrong."

"And so you avoided confrontations?"

"Right," she replied.

"Like you avoid them now, with John?"

"I suppose. Yes. I do the same thing with him that I did with them."

"Is that true sexually, also? Are you avoiding sex for some reason?"

Laura thought about it. "Maybe," she said. "When John comes on to me sexually, I feel myself tighten up. I want to pull away. I don't know why, but you're right, I am avoiding it."

"I've noticed," I said, "that when you and John are here together, you seem intimidated by him. He speaks up, but you don't. In fact, judging by the expression on your face, I'd say you were afraid of him."

"I guess that's true," said Laura. "In some ways—maybe a lot of ways—John is like my father. And I relate to him the same way. That's not so good, is it?"

Laura's insight into her situation proved to be very accurate. In some ways, John really was like her father. For one thing, though he claimed to be supportive and said he wanted her self-esteem to improve, in actuality he was very critical of her. He wanted things done his way, and he wanted her personality and their relationship to fit his expectations. Most of her own self-doubts were reflected in his attitudes toward her. He was critical of the way she handled the children, the way she ran the house, her aspirations for the future. He expressed doubts about her basic character, saying, for example, that she was immature and untrustworthy. Then he was puzzled by why she didn't want to make love to him!

I've met many men and women whose situations are similar to Laura's. On the surface, the problems in their relationships have to do with their lack of interest in sex. Beneath that surface, though, and underlying the problem of sexual desire, are issues related to power and control. These people tend to feel power- less and intimidated. In some cases, they have relationships with partners who are very controlling and who want to be domi- nant. In other cases, the problem is more their own, in the sense that they are too timid to assert themselves. And sometimes the truth is somewhere in the middle. In any case, the goal—the "cure" for the problem—is the same. It has to do with learning to express thoughts and feelings, to confront issues, and to *share power* in a relationship. Once this can begin to happen, holding back seems to stop, and sexual passion begins to reappear.

How can you tell if feelings of powerlessness are playing a role in the decline of your sex life? There are certain signs that you can look for. The more of these signs you find, the more likely it is that powerlessness is playing a role in your frustra- tions. Ask yourself the following questions:

- Which one of you has "lost" your interest in sex?
- Was there a time when that person was more interested in sex, and more aggressive about it?
- Does the person who's lost interest in sex also have prob- lems of self-esteem, meaning that they doubt themselves all the time, have trouble making decisions, are unassertive, can't say "no," and tend to feel that they're always in the wrong?
- Do you find yourselves avoiding fights and conflicts? Who is the one who seems to want to avoid issues rather than confronting them?
- Are there long periods of silence and withdrawal following conflicts in your relationship?

Much of the material in later chapters will be of use to people who need to overcome problems related to power in relation- ships. Much of this work has to do with building self-esteem, learning to trust, and learning to negotiate and compromise. As you'll see, all of these things have a great impact on intimacy and sexual desire. They have a great deal to do with staying in love, versus falling out of love.

Sparks and Fires: Sexual Fantasy and Sexual Desire

"Let me ask you something, Doctor."

The redheaded woman crossed her legs and folded her arms. She was pretty, with the kind of rosy, freckled complexion that redheads often have. She had a nice figure, too. She was wearing a skirt and blouse that complemented her colouring. I could smell her perfume clear across the room. Looking into her violet eyes, I felt my heartbeat quicken just a little.

As nice as she was to look at, I didn't think my client had dressed for me. In fact, I was pretty sure that if it was aimed at anyone, her effort was aimed at the man who sat beside her. I'd encountered this scenario before: a woman dressed in a way that could provoke sexual thoughts and feelings in a lot of men, *except* in the one man it was intended for.

Frustrated efforts to get a sexual rise from an unresponsive partner are awful experiences. You can imagine how it undermines a person's self-esteem to try deliberately to turn someone on but then to get no response. Though it might not be intended that way, the lack of reaction comes across as a cruel rejection. If that kind of situation goes on long enough, the frustration can turn into a bitter resentment that erodes the fabric of a marriage. It was getting dangerously close to that, I thought, for Alice and Bill. If she wasn't yet close to divorce, she was at least getting to the point where it could be tempting to pick up on some other man's interest. When you're feeling really low, that kind of temptation can be hard to resist.

Alice continued. "Is it normal," she asked, "for a man never to think about sex? I mean, *never*? Bill tells me that's the way he is. He can be away from me for a week, not touch me for a month, and never once in that time does he even *think* about sex. Maybe I'm oversexed—tell me if I am—but it seems to me that I think about sex pretty often. I get horny, you know? I know other women who do, too. And men. But Bill doesn't, and that just doesn't seem normal. I wonder sometimes if it's me—if he just isn't turned on to me. He says that's not true, but I still wonder about it."

I thought it was important for Alice to get things off her chest, so I let her go on. I thought it was important, too, for Bill to hear her out, no matter how uncomfortable it made him.

"At home, I can put on a sexy nightgown and perfume. I can walk around stark naked for that matter. But it's like he's blind! Now tell me, is that normal?"

Alice shook her head in exasperation. Something about the anger in her voice made me uneasy. It ran through my mind again that here was a woman who could be dangerously close to looking for a response outside of her marriage, if for no other reason than her own self-respect. It was clear that she believed she'd tried hard, had done everything she could think of, but was getting nowhere. She sounded like someone who was close to the end of her tether. I hoped that we could get Bill to respond to her, and soon.

To those who do find themselves thinking about sex and feeling horny now and then, it may seem hard to believe that there are people who don't. It's true, though. Some men and women— maybe more than you'd suspect—don't indulge in sexual fantasies, or let themselves enjoy the kinds of sexy feelings that are a part of everyday life for others. Not surprisingly, these people are often out of touch with their sexual desire.

The following questions can provide you with some useful food for thought. Take a minute or two to answer them before reading on.

Sexual Fantasy Inventory

- How often do you find yourself having sexy thoughts or fantasies?
- Do you have favourite sexual fantasies that you enjoy over and over again?
- Do you notice yourself reacting with a sexy feeling or thought in response to things you see or hear in the course of an average day?
- When you do find yourself having a sexy thought, or feeling, do you let it run through your mind for a while, more or less savouring it, to turn your mind to other things right away?
- Would you feel embarrassed or ashamed to admit to a friend that you enjoyed sexual fantasies?
- Do you sometimes get turned on by a sexy passage in a book? How about sexy scenes in a movie?
- Do you ever indulge in sexual fantasies when you make love?

People who are in touch with their sexual passion *do* think about sex, and often. They let themselves respond to all sorts of sexual cues in their environment: passages in books and magazines, scenes in movies and on television, and things about the people they see every day. They enjoy sexy feelings, fantasies, and daydreams. For them the world is full of sights, sounds, even smells that provoke sexual thoughts and stir up sexy feelings. They don't necessarily tell anyone about these feelings, much less act on them all the time, but they do *enjoy* them. As one woman said to me, "I like my sexy feelings. I like to let them simmer inside me. I stir the pot every once in a while, keeping it warm until I get home to my husband. It's like making stew: it gets better the longer it simmers!"

Sexual desire doesn't pop out of thin air. It comes from inside us. Usually it begins as a spark; it rarely comes on as a full-blown flame. Though occasionally it may be a wave that sweeps us away, more often sexual passion is a fire that we build from more modest beginnings. Typically it begins as a *thought or feeling* that we have in reaction to something we see, hear, or smell. Sexual fantasy is one way to take a spark of sexual desire and build it into a flame of passion. Sexual fantasy is also something we can use to strike a spark. Finally, sexual fantasy is a tool we can use to keep sexual interest "simmering" until the time is right to act on it.

People who complain that they have little sexual desire may be people who react to the flickers and sparks of their own sexuality not with excitement, but with guilt or anxiety. Instead of enjoying those feelings, of flowing with them, they often do just the opposite: they avoid them and turn their minds purposely to other things. No wonder there's usually nothing simmering when they get home!

People who accept their own sexuality don't avoid sexual fantasies. On the contrary, they often enjoy them so much that they cultivate favourites. They use these tried and true fantasies whenever they want to strike a spark, turn a flame into a fire, or keep a warm feeling alive.

Body Images

Draw a picture of yourself naked. Go ahead, try it.

Does that suggestion make you uncomfortable? If so, then chances are you have some uncomfortable feelings about your body, or what we more technically refer to as a poor *body image*.

A person's body image is related to his or her overall self-esteem in a very simple and direct way. Our opinion of ourselves—whether we feel pride or shame—has its deepest roots in two areas: our bodies and our minds. Primary sources for building pride include our intellect and our sensitivity, our skills and our appearance. People with low self-esteem always believe they are lacking in one or more of these areas. Regardless of what others may think, they believe they're stupid or insensitive, clumsy or ugly.

People whose low self-esteem is rooted primarily in one area often try to cover it up by emphasizing and developing one they feel better about. People can be very effective at this, so much so that it can be a real shock to discover that someone you thought was very together really has severe problems of self-esteem that they have been keeping under wraps for years. It is particularly common for someone to try to make up for a poor body image through material success, status, or power. Sometimes the very people you would expect to have the best body images—people who take special pains about their appearance—are secretly very critical of the way they look and insecure about their attractiveness.

Regardless of how well they cover it up or compensate for it, people become self-conscious and defensive because of their low self-esteem. A poor body image also has a way of interfering with a person's social development. Especially during adolescence, when most of us are pretty self-conscious, severe doubts and anxieties about our bodies can alienate us from others and make us feel that life is passing us by. The result is an immature, anxious individual.

In today's body-conscious world, it is an unusual person who doesn't have at least some mixed feelings about the way he or she looks. Everyone thinks they are either too short or too tall, too fat or too skinny. We are embarrassed about every gray hair and wrinkle. We wish we had different breasts, different thighs, different hair, or different noses. These kinds of anxieties may be a problem, but they seem almost normal these days.

The difference between "normal" worry about appearance, and really harmful body-image problems, is a matter of degree. There can be a fine line between the two, and many of us probably venture across it now and then, depending on our situation. To get some feeling for where you are right now, try answering the following questions:

Body Image Inventory

- Do you feel comfortable wearing clothes that draw attention to yourself?
- How do you feel about being seen in a bathing suit?
- Do you enjoy shopping for new clothes?
- Do you feel comfortable having someone take a picture of you? .
- Do you exercise regularly?
- Are you careful about nutrition?
- Do you diet repeatedly, losing and re-gaining weight over and over again?
- When you look in the mirror, are you pretty comfortable with what you see or very critical of yourself?

People with poor body images usually don't like shopping for clothes or wearing clothes that draw attention to themselves. They would sooner fade into the wallpaper than stand out in a crowd. They are never satisfied with the way they look, and they often abuse their bodies, with poor eating habits or crash dieting, for example. They don't exercise regularly, and they may abuse all sorts of drugs, from diet pills to cocaine.

To test out your body image even further, take off your clothes and look at yourself in a full-length mirror. (If you don't have a full-length mirror, what do you think that says about your body image?)

As you look at yourself in the mirror, do you feel comfortable or uncomfortable? What parts of yourself do your eyes want to avoid? Can you find at least as many things that you like about your body as you dislike about it? Is it easy, or difficult, to imagine someone being sexually attracted to what you see in the mirror? Look at your genitals. Can you imagine someone being attracted to that part of yourself?

People with low sexual desire often have severe body-image problems. They tend to have especially negative attitudes about their sex organs. They may think their genitals are ugly, or inadequate in some way. They may dislike themselves so much that they don't even like being touched, much less being made love to. You simply can't feel good about getting physically close to someone else when you don't feel okay about yourself. If you have a really poor body image, you probably don't want to make love.

Gender-Role Conflict

"I remember wishing that I was a boy. I always was a tomboy, as far back as I can recall. I suppose in some ways I still am."

Does this describe you or someone you know? It isn't all that unusual for a man to have mixed feelings at times about being a man, or for a woman to feel conflicted about being a woman. When it becomes habitual, though, inner conflict over being male or female leads to problems.

"Gender-role conflict" refers to the inner conflict that a person can have over their sex. Often it is a sign of a body-image problem. When you talk with them, these people often doubt their "masculinity" or "femininity." They feel inadequately equipped to play the role of a man or a woman as they see it— physically, emotionally, or both. In its milder forms, gender-role conflict undermines sexual desire by making us feel inadequate. It undermines intimacy by making us feel different and ashamed. In its more severe forms, gender-role conflict leads people to want to change sexes.

The woman who made the statement above had always thought of herself as "boyish." Physically, instead of being soft and petite, her physique had always been large and muscular. While her girlfriends were developing breasts and curving figures, her chest stayed disappointingly flat, her body lines uncomfortably straight. While their interests turned to clothes, make-up, and boys, hers turned to competitive sports.

I didn't totally agree with Peggy's assessment of herself as "unfeminine." Though I could see why she would come to think of herself that way, she also had many distinctly feminine qualities. I noticed that whenever I pointed out something about her that struck me as feminine, though, she would act very uncomfortable. She would fidget in her chair and look annoyed. It was as if she had decided that she was masculine. My suggesting anything to the contrary bothered her.

I pointed out these negative reactions to Peggy. I told her how it seemed to me that she found it annoying that I could see her as being feminine. I then took a further risk and pointed out how I thought she actually exaggerated her "masculine" appearance. For example, her wardrobe consisted almost exclusively of baggy jeans and flannel shirts. I asked if she had ever thought of wearing jewellery, or trying some make-up, or putting on something besides baggy jeans and faded flannel shirts. My perception of her, I said, was of someone who was trying to hide the fact that she was a woman.

That last comment got a reaction. Peggy got good and mad. But as it turned out, it also opened the door to some productive talking. It cleared the air and paved the way for a much greater degree of frankness and honesty in our conversations.

People like Peg, who are experiencing gender-role conflict, are often suspected of being gay or lesbian. These suspicions, which usually are inaccurate, are fuelled by the fact that the people in question often have a low sex drive. Their disinterest in making love with the opposite sex, however, doesn't necessarily mean that they would be any more interested in going to bed with someone of the same sex. They are out of touch with their sexuality, full stop.

Gender-role conflict isn't the same as "sexual-orientation conflict," which means inner struggles over *who* you're attracted to— people of the same sex or people of the opposite sex. Gender-role conflict refers to the mixed feelings a person can have about the *role* they believe they are expected to play in the social world at large. Their mixed feelings are usually a reflection of a sense of inadequacy about their ability to meet those expectations. Usually, they also have negative feelings about "manhood," or "womanhood," in general. That was certainly true for Peg. Aside from the fact that she always thought of herself as physically unfeminine, she also had distinctly negative feelings about what she saw as the second-class role of women in society. She hated the idea of being born a second-class citizen, relatively powerless and an object of discrimination in what was basically a man's world. The idea of conforming to that role made her sick at heart. So, she rejected the role, and along with it she rejected her femininity. She had relationships with men, but found herself unsexual in them. She was distant and guarded, and the relationships rarely lasted long.

To understand the problems created by gender-role conflict, we need to examine the sex roles that we socialize men and women to fulfil. These sex roles, after all, are the basis for relationships. If staying in love has a lot to do with how we structure our relationships, then we need to be careful about how we do that. Do we want simply to swallow whole the sex roles we modelled as we grew up, or do we want to build our relationships on something different? We need to answer questions like these for ourselves:

- Are the models of sexual desirability that we present to our children—in magazines and in books, in movies and on television—healthy ideals for them to be striving for?
- Are our ideals of sexuality—the *macho man*, and the *foxy lady*—effective models for building intimacy and sustaining sexual desire in a relationship over the years?
- What do men have to give up in order to be *macho*, and what do women sacrifice in order to be *foxy*? How much of themselves do they need to keep hidden in order to maintain these images?

Partners

Phil and Anne came for help because Anne wasn't interested in sex. At the time, they hadn't made love in three years. She owned up to the problem right away. It was all her fault, she said. In her opinion, Phil had every right to be angry.

From the outset I noticed that Anne was determined to find some *physical* reason for her lack of sexual desire. I figured that was because a physical cause would let her off the hook, allowing her to write off the situation as hopeless. So when she said, "I think there's something wrong with my skin," I had my doubts, but I went along with her and asked her to describe it. "Whenever Philip touches me, I start to feel real uncomfortable. It starts right away, with the first touch. Pretty soon it's almost painful, and afterward I develop a rash that can last for days."

It isn't so unusual for people who are anxious about sex to say that being touched feels uncomfortable. Some say that they are ticklish, while others say that being touched makes their skin crawl. The cause of this is anxiety. I tried explaining this to Anne, but, as I suspected, she wasn't very interested in what I had to say. She frowned when I suggested that it might be nervous tension, rather than some rare and mysterious skin disease or allergy, that accounted for her reaction.

Anne started off our next session talking about sex hormones. She had been doing some reading, she said, and it seemed to her that the problem must be that she was deficient in some hormone. She must not have enough of whatever chemical it was that made people interested in sex. I said that wasn't likely, and again she seemed annoyed.

In our third session, Anne shifted her focus again, this time from sex hormones and sensitive skin to her uterus and problems with her menstrual cycle. She went into elaborate detail about her discomfort. I soon got an idea of what she was leading up to. Finally she said it. "Things have just been so bad, for so long, that last week I spoke with my gynaecologist about a hysterectomy."

"What did he say?" I asked.

"Well, he thinks I'm kind of young. He wants me to think about it for a while. But to tell you the truth, my mind's pretty well made up. As far as I'm concerned, I've suffered with the thing long enough. The sooner it's out, the better."

I didn't doubt that Anne might be having menstrual discomfort, but I was bothered by the fact that she was willing to settle on a hysterectomy so quickly. I suspected that if she went ahead with the operation she could use it as an excuse for permanently avoiding sex. I knew from my own clinical experience and from research reports I had read, that her interest in an early hysterectomy could be a sign that she was close to giving up on sex altogether. There is good evidence that a hysterectomy *doesn't* have a negative influence on sex drive, *except* in women who had little interest beforehand. For that group, sex does tend to drop off after a hysterectomy. I had good reason to suspect, therefore, that if Anne went through with her plan, Phil could find himself without a sexual partner on a permanent basis.

Anne's ambivalence about her own sexuality was the most obvious aspect of this case. Yet it was also only *one* aspect of it. It would have been easy to lay all the blame for Phil and Anne's sexual troubles at her doorstep. After all, she was so up front with her complaints, so obviously ambivalent about sex, that it would have been tempting to ignore Phil altogether. That would have been tempting, too, because whenever I tried asking a question or two about his sexuality, he'd get uptight, start fidgeting in his chair, and blush deeply. At those times Anne would quickly jump in, diverting the conversation back to herself. Then, instead of talking about some aspect of Philip's sexuality, I'd suddenly find myself talking to Anne about her sex hormones, her sensitive skin, or her menstrual cramps.

It was only through stubborn persistence that I eventually learned that Phil had a history of premature ejaculation, and that this had made intercourse frustrating for Anne. What's more, I discovered that he was a person who was very uptight about sex, maybe even more uptight than Anne. He had a long list of sexual *do's* and *don'ts,* which was overloaded with things that he wasn't willing to do in bed. He imposed these limits on his lovemaking with Anne. While he talked on the one hand about being open and flexible, when it came right down to it he was very limited in what he felt comfortable with, and he was very resistant to trying anything new. But whenever I tried to talk about it, up came his defences, and in came Anne's distractions.

On the surface, then, and especially in comparison to Anne's very apparent hang-ups, Phil's sexual conflicts may have seemed minor. If I hadn't pressed the issue, his problems may never have come to light. This is something that happens a lot: a person with a very obvious problem can act as a shield for someone who is too insecure to look at himself. In Phil's case, that anxiety and insecurity was there, lurking just below the surface, and it was intense. It had a lot to do with body-image problems that he had kept secret, even from Anne. His self-esteem in general wasn't particularly good, and he had a hard time trusting someone enough to be vulnerable with them.

Partners of people who have lost their interest in sex often have sexual conflicts of their own. Their conflicts may be less obvious, but these conflicts can play a big role in the sexual frustrations that a couple is having together. In truth, people like Phil can be attracted to people like Anne *because* their own sexual anxieties and insecurities can be more or less safely hidden behind someone else's more obvious hang-ups. Once Phil and I developed a deep level of trust in our relationship, Phil admitted that one thing he had liked about Anne from the beginning was that she wasn't as sexually aggressive as some of the other women he had known. "Looking back on it, I'd have to admit that I liked the fact that she was sexually shy," he said. "It let me be the one in control. I can remember feeling some relief at that." That admission took courage. I told Phil that I admired him for being willing to face up to that part of himself. It turned out to be a real turning point, too, not only for him alone, but for him and Anne.

If you are in a relationship with someone who has lost their interest in sex, gradually or suddenly, take the time to ask yourself the following questions. They can help to get you in touch with issues within yourself that may be contributing, in some way and in some degree, to the problems you are having together. I am not suggesting that you should shoulder all the responsibility for these problems. I am only suggesting that you may need to shoulder part of it. To build a better sex life, both you and your partner may need to do some changing.

- Name three things about *your partner's* sexual attitudes or behaviour that you would like to see change.
- Name three things about *your own* sexual attitudes or behaviour that you would like to change.
- How do you think the material in each section of this chapter might apply to *you*, as well as to your partner?

3

Intimate Relationships

In the last chapter, we looked at some of the issues that can cause sexual desire to deteriorate. In this chapter, we focus in on intimacy, on the *conditions* that make intimacy possible and that keep it alive.

Power and Intimacy

True intimacy depends on equality. It's a fact that people will hesitate to be completely open with someone whom they perceive as having control over them, or whom they think is in a position to judge them. Nothing is more vital to intimacy than a feeling of equality and acceptance in a relationship. Equality and acceptance facilitate intimacy; inequality suppresses it.

Differences in power—either perceived or real—are the reason why people will often talk more openly to a friend or a therapist than to a parent, a supervisor, or, sadly, even a spouse. A good friend is in the position of helper, not judge. A good friend does not try to run your life. There is a sense of acceptance and equality in a good friendship. These kinds of relationships, built on a foundation of trust, are conducive to openness and intimacy. The same must be true for a marriage, if we want it to be intimate.

What is intimacy? Basically it has to do with communication, with sharing and openness. Intimate relationships are open relationships. Partners who say they feel intimate with each other also say that they can be open *to* each other, that they keep few if any secrets. They tell things to each other and reveal parts of themselves that they don't ordinarily share with others. They dare to be spontaneous and playful with each other. They are unguarded with each other. They have individual goals, and individual lives, but they also have a shared future that they believe in deeply, and a shared life where they find joy and serenity. In intimate relationships there is a profound sense of involvement, a feeling of connectedness, a sense of a joining of souls. The relationship has a life of its own. It co-exists with the two individuals who make it up, living alongside them as sort of a third person, taking nourishment from the intimacy that binds them.

Problems of intimacy almost always involve problems of trust, of acceptance, and ultimately, of equality. Problems of intimacy suggest problems of power. Trust will be discussed more later; for now let's focus on acceptance and equality. Answer the following questions:

- Do you feel that your partner accepts you as you are, or do you feel that your partner has a lot of reservations about the kind of person you are?
- Do you often find yourself feeling critical of your partner's attitudes or behaviour?
- Do you feel that the decisions in your relationship are made together, or does one of you seem to have more say-so than the other?
- Do you feel equal, superior, or inferior to your partner in terms of how much power and influence you have in your relationship?

Relationships that are *egalitarian* are relationships that have achieved a great deal of mutual acceptance, and where partners feel that they have more or less equal say-so in what goes on—not necessarily on every issue, but overall. This kind of relationship, and only this kind of relationship, is one in which intimacy can deepen and grow over time. Relationships that lack this essential egalitarian quality are fated to be less intimate.

How can you tell if a problem of acceptance or power is undermining or limiting intimacy in your relationship? You can tell because . . .

One of you will feel judged or criticized by the other,
and
One of you will probably feel that the other has more power in the relationship.

The result of being in a relationship where one partner feels superior to the other, and where one partner has most of the power, is that sooner or later the one who is the underdog will begin to hold back. Over time that person will become less open, less communicative, more guarded and alienated. Eventually, she or he will start keeping secrets and building resentments. Rather than trying to get what they want by being direct and assertive, people who feel judged and powerless will try to get it indirectly. This doesn't make them feel very good about themselves. Often they feel guilty and angry with themselves. But it may be the only way they know to get what they want.

In one relationship I observed, problems of acceptance and power were painfully obvious, though it took some time for the couple to see it for themselves. Martin and Kate had been married for almost twenty years, and for the last ten they had been growing further apart. Kate's interest in making love had gone steadily downhill. They spent less and less time together, and they felt less and less close.

Kate was a bright and energetic woman whose self-esteem had been growing ever since she started working and going back to school to complete a college degree that had been left incomplete. She was still, however, a very shy and somewhat timid woman, who preferred to avoid fights rather than confront issues and clear the air. She had been this way ever since she was a child, and she attributed these qualities to being raised by a demanding and critical mother. "No matter what I did, what I looked like, Mother would always find something wrong. She always seemed to find something to criticize. I found myself avoiding her as much as possible. To this day I don't feel we have a real relationship. We see each other fairly often, now that Dad is gone, but I swear she doesn't know the least bit about who I really am, what I'm really like. I just won't reveal myself to her."

When she met Martin, at age twenty, Kate was impressed by his intelligence and self-confidence. He pursued her and eventually won her over. She left college. They got married and had two children, and for a few years all went well between them. Kate stayed home with the kids, while Martin worked hard and got ahead.

The problems started, Kate said, after the second baby was born. "It was then that I started feeling resentful of Martin. He expected me to take care of two kids virtually by myself, and then to take care of him, too."

"How do you mean?" I asked. "Take care of him how?"

"Every way," she replied. "Sexually, emotionally, physically—you name it. I don't think I realized it consciously then, but I think I began to see sex as a burden. It was something that I had to do to satisfy Martin. He was very verbal about it. He wouldn't hesitate to nag me for sex. I'd finally give in—it's always been difficult for me not to give in to Martin—and fake it as best I could. He didn't seem to mind. Turns out he never suspected that I was faking it. But the truth was I'd lay there thinking about the laundry that had to be done. It couldn't be over fast enough for me."

If the past had simply been the past, I think that Kate might have been able to work through her bad feelings about sex. Her resentment toward Martin for being an uninvolved parent and a demanding lover might have dwindled. After all, she admitted that she was partly to blame. Her own passivity—her unwillingness to confront Martin and to try to change things—had played a role in the problem.

But the past wasn't the past, as was evident in the way Martin and Kate related to each other in our sessions. Martin had a judgmental attitude toward Kate. He talked a lot, but didn't listen much. He was quick to criticize, and slow to praise. In our talks, he kept referring to her "frigidity." I'd see her frown whenever he'd use that word, but, true to form, she'd never confront him.

Martin's critical attitude, combined with Kate's passivity, had created a climate of inequality in their marriage that had become a barrier between them. Kate was resentful. Feeling inferior and one-down made it difficult for her to open up to Martin. To be able to rebuild their marriage, to rediscover intimacy, and to help rekindle Kate's sexual desire, this couple had to work on overcoming the inequality that stood in the way of closeness and passion. They needed to work toward building a more egalitarian relationship. Kate needed to learn to be more assertive with her feelings and willing to confront issues instead of avoiding them. That was the only way she could change the balance of power in her marriage and feel more equal to Martin. He, on the other hand, had to deal with his anxieties about sharing power as well as his inclination to sit in judgment of his wife. If these things could happen, I felt I could assure them that their marriage could get better; if not, I wasn't so sure about their chances of feeling closer, or of Kate recapturing her sexual interest in Martin.

Self-Esteem, Intimacy, and Sexual Desire

When we think of someone with self-esteem, we think of a person who likes him- or herself. That might be a bit oversimplified, but it's basically an accurate definition of self-esteem. Self-esteem has to do with our attitude toward ourselves, with the extent to which we appreciate our assets, accept our liabilities, and respect ourselves. Self-esteem exerts a tremendous influence in our relationships. It plays a particularly important role in intimacy. And last but not least, it greatly influences our ability to change.

Intimacy is critical to sexual desire in long-term relationships; self-esteem facilitates intimacy. Therefore, self-esteem is something we need to deal with. To get in touch with your own level of self-esteem, try answering the questions listed below.

Self-Esteem Inventory

- Name five things about yourself that you're most proud of.

For each of the following pairs of statements, choose the *one* that comes closest to summarizing your own feelings or opinions:

(a) In the long run, people get the respect and rewards they earn in life.

OR

(b) Unfortunately, an individual's worth often passes unrecognized no matter how hard he or she tries.

(a) Becoming a success is mostly a matter of hard work and persistence.

OR

(b) Getting ahead in life is mainly a matter of luck.

(a) My future is in my own hands.

OR

(b) My future will be the result of forces beyond my control.

For each of the following statements, do you agree or disagree?

- Most people seem to be more assertive than me.
- People often take advantage of me.
- When it comes down to choosing between what I want and what someone else wants, I'm usually the one who gives in.

- I have a hard time saying no.
- I make a lot of sacrifices to please others, but others rarely sacrifice anything for me.
- In my relationships, it's the other person who's usually in control.
- I have what it takes to be a success in life.
- I feel depressed a lot of the time.
- Most of the time when I really want something, I find a way to get it.

As you can tell from looking at the range of questions in this short inventory, self-esteem is actually a pretty complex thing. But boiled down, it has a lot to do with having confidence in yourself, standing by yourself, and getting what you want out of life. It means believing in your own basic equality to others— in your right to pursue happiness. It means having confidence in your ability to achieve that happiness. People who have self-esteem have a sense of personal power; they believe in their ability to influence the course of their own lives. They believe they have some control over what happens to them, as well as the right to exercise that control. They believe that personal effort can make a difference in a person's life, between success and failure, between fulfillment and frustration. They can be as considerate and caring as the next person, but they don't always put others ahead of themselves. Most of the time they go after what they want, and keep after it. They don't go out of their way to hurt anyone, but they recognize that there are times when a person might have to disappoint or hurt someone in order to take care of themselves.

The men and women I meet who strike me as the most healthy, psychologically speaking, are those who feel some basic pride in themselves, not just in the way they look, what they can do, or what they have, but *who they are*. They believe that they're equal to others, and that they have as much right to get what they want out of life as anyone else does. They truly believe that they're worthwhile—valuable as friends and lovers, and deserving of respect and consideration.

Having self-esteem sets the stage for getting more of what you want out of life. In contrast, low self-esteem leads to its own vicious cycle, where you get less and feel worse. When you have self-esteem, you are more likely to maintain some sense of balance in your relationships between giving and taking, and to do something about it when you feel that things are getting out of balance. In other words, you are more likely to want an equal relationship and to feel unhappy if that's not what you have. You might be willing to give more than you get for a while, depending on the circumstances, but you won't put up with that forever. At the same time, when you have self-esteem you are apt to be less defensive and more open to change and compromise.

Naturally, no one I know has a perfect self-image, a totally invulnerable sense of self-esteem. As with body-images, everyone has their weak spots. The difference between someone who has good self-esteem and someone who doesn't is that the one with better self-esteem spends less time depressed and takes a more active role in getting what he or she wants. They find ways to take care of themselves in a crisis. The person with poor self-esteem, in contrast, often feels helpless and depressed, tends to be rigid and defensive, and can become paralyzed in times of crisis. Probably the saddest thing about people with low self-esteem is the way they hold themselves back. They often don't achieve their goals in life, either because they don't try at all, or because they give up too easily. They usually have very little idea of what they want. They set their expectations too low, and therefore they get very little. In some sense, people with low self-esteem suffer from problems of identity. That's because knowing *who we are* depends to some extent on knowing *what we want*. When we don't know what we want, we usually aren't sure who we are.

In relationships, low self-esteem stands as a barrier to equality, and therefore to openness and intimacy. Instead of being put down by others, people with low self-esteem put themselves one-down. They feel inferior, and they act inferior. They either avoid conflicts and confrontation altogether, or else refuse compromise. They avoid communication, won't listen and won't change. They stifle growth in their relationships.

Trust and Intimacy

To discover whether you're basically a trusting or distrusting person, answer the following questions true or false:

Trust Inventory

1. People can usually be counted on to keep their promises.
2. You need to be careful or someone is likely to take advantage of you.
3. Most people would cheat or steal if they thought they could get away with it.
4. Most idealists are sincere and try their best to practice what they preach.
5. Most people can be trusted to tell the truth.
6. Depending on others is a good way to get hurt.

Here are the "trusting" answers to the above questions: 1) true; 2) false; 3) false; 4) true; 5) true; 6) false. How do your responses compare? Are you relatively trusting, distrusting, or somewhere in the middle?

There is some reason to believe that people in general may be less trusting today than in generations before. We're living in times when there is widespread scepticism about many social institutions, including marriage. People have lost faith and are doubtful about the chances for commitment and monogamy working over the long run.

On the brighter side, there is hard evidence that people who are able to trust may have some advantages over those who can't. For example, did you know that . . .

- people who are more trusting are *less* likely to lie?
- people who *dis*trust are *more* likely to cheat if an opportunity comes their way?
- trusting persons are seen by others as *happier* than people who are distrustful?
- trusting persons are seen as coming from better *adjusted* families, and as having *happier* childhoods?
- people are more interested in being *friends* with someone who trusts?
- people who trust are more likely to give someone else a second chance?
- people who can trust tend to score better on tests of overall *adjustment* than people who are distrustful?

Considering what these statements say about the advantages of being a person who trusts, it's ironic that we sometimes stereotype people who are trusting as gullible, naïve, or just plain dumb. In reality, people who trust are no less intelligent than anyone else; neither are they more naïve or gullible. They aren't any more easy to fool than the next person, and may actually be less easy to fool. They learn from experience, and will stop trusting someone who has let them down too many times. A distrustful person, on the other hand, may actually be more vulnerable of being the victim of a con game. Why? Because the distrustful person is more willing to cheat, and is therefore liable to get taken in by someone who is better at it than they are.

People who trust seem to take the attitude that others can and should be counted on *unless* there is some good reason to think otherwise. Distrustful people take just the opposite approach. They believe you need proof *before* you trust anyone in the first place. Depending on how distrustful they are, they may never get enough proof to convince them to take a chance, to open up and have faith in someone else.

❦   ❦   ❦

Being able to trust relates very directly to intimacy. Intimacy means getting close. It means opening up, which means being vulnerable. Intimacy is a testimony to faith in a relationship. Instead of opening up and risking that vulnerability, of taking that leap of faith, distrustful people play it close to the vest in relationships. They hold back. Typically they spend a lot of time finding fault with others, to justify their distrust. Since few of us are saints, it isn't hard to find minor faults in just about anyone. Distrustful people act as if these normal human imperfections were something more than that. They try to make you feel guilty about being normal, about having normal faults and flaws. If you don't take this bait, though, you can see through this smokescreen into the distrustful person's real motive: they are finding fault in order to put you on the defensive and give themselves a good excuse for not opening up, being honest, or having faith in you.

One man I saw seemed hopelessly entangled in a web of distrust that had just about destroyed his marriage. To describe Brian as ambitious would be an understatement; he was downright driven. He was also extremely successful. In many ways he was the kind of man that many other men envy and that a lot of women are attracted to. He cut a dashing figure: handsome and bright, stylish, athletic, and self-confident. To others he must have seemed like he had the world by the tail. But that was just the view from a distance. Up close, his friends and closest associates had a different opinion. They found him cold and unapproachable. His wife, Edie, had felt shut out sexually, emotionally, and intellectually for years. They came to see me because she was at the point where she had finally threatened a divorce.

When I met with him alone, Brian expressed fears that a divorce would leave him financially devastated. I asked him about his feelings for Edie. Was he upset about the idea of losing her?

"Of course I am," he replied. "I love Edie." But his voice sounded hollow, and in the awkward silence that followed we found ourselves sitting there staring at each other.

"I have to confess," he said finally, "that personally I've never had much faith in psychologists, or in therapy." Somehow I wasn't surprised.

I asked Brian why he'd decided to come in. "Well, you heard Edie—she says she'll divorce me if I don't make an effort. And I figure that if it ever does come down to that, and we end up in a courtroom, it would look bad for me if I refused to see you."

As Brian and I began to go over his personal history, I learned that Edie wasn't the only person he'd had trouble getting close to. He was fundamentally suspicious of everyone. In his marriage, his distrust had become a wall that separated him from his wife. He couldn't appreciate how it might feel to be on the other side of that wall, on the receiving end of his distrust.

I brought up the subject of trust. Brian struck me, I told him, as a man of little faith, who was deeply distrustful and profoundly sceptical. He owned up to that. He actually seemed proud of it, in fact. "You don't think I got where I am by *trusting* everyone, do you?" he asked with a smile.

"I don't know about that," I replied, "but where do you think that attitude has got you in your marriage?"

He thought about it. "Maybe it hasn't helped," he conceded. Then he looked me in the eye. "Are you suggesting that that's the problem in my marriage?"

I smiled. He was, I thought, a bright man. Maybe there was some hope for him.

How can you tell if problems of trust are undermining your relationship? Some of the key signs can be found in your answers to the following quiz.

1. Does your partner accuse you of untrustworthiness?
2. How do you and your partner handle your personal finances?
   • We have separate savings and current accounts.
   • We have joint savings and current accounts.
   • We have a joint account for most things, plus smaller separate accounts.
3. If something is bothering or worrying your partner, would they be inclined to . . .

- Talk to you about it, or
- Keep their worries and concerns to themselves?
4. Does your partner frequently make major purchases without telling you first?
5. Does your partner talk to you about decisions . . .
   - *before* they are made, or
   - only *after* they are made, if at all?
6. If your partner goes out without you, does he/she . . .
   - tell you where they're going, and when they'll be back, or
   - just say they're going out?
7. Does your partner become angry at being asked where he or she has been, who they were with, or what they were doing?
8. Does your partner volunteer a lot of information about what goes on in his or her day, or do you usually have to ask a lot of questions to get much information?
9. Can you tell pretty easily what your partner is feeling or thinking, or does he/she keep thoughts and feelings more or less secret?

It shouldn't be hard to figure out which answers go along with a relationship where there is trust and intimacy and which answers point the way to distrust and lack of intimacy. After answering these questions about your *partner*, it would be helpful to go through them a second time, this time replacing the word "partner" with the word "you." How much do *you* trust your partner? How much might *you* be contributing to problems of intimacy in your relationship?

Building and maintaining trust is a crucial issue for relationships. Trust lies at the core of an intimate relationship. A relationship based on trust is the only kind of relationship that can truly grow with time. It's the only kind of relationship in which intimacy can deepen, and it's the only kind of relationship that can sustain sexual passion over the years. This is the kind of relationship that most people, in their hearts, have yearned for over the generations.

The following words describe that yearning more eloquently than most:

That there should exist one other person in the world towards whom all openness of interchange should establish itself, from whom there should be no concealment; whose body should be as dear to one, in every part, as one's own; with whom there should be no sense of Mine or Thine, in property or possession; into whose mind one's thoughts should naturally flow, as it were to know themselves and receive a new illumination; and between whom and oneself there should be a spontaneous rebound of sympathy in all the joys and sorrows and experiences of life; such is perhaps one of the dearest wishes of the soul.

Love's Coming of Age
EDWARD CARPENTER, 1896

The words may be old, but the feelings they express are as fresh today as the day they were written. They're the same feelings that burn in the hearts of men and women today, just as they did a century ago. Edward Carpenter's description of intimacy reaches out to us across time. The people I work with express these same sentiments, perhaps less eloquently, but no less sincerely. They want this closeness and connectedness to another person that he wrote about. Trust and self-esteem are the foundation of this kind of intimacy.

4

I'm Too Old for That,
and Other Myths About
Intimacy and Passion

In this chapter we're going to do some mental housecleaning. We're going to sweep out some cobwebs. We're going to let some fresh air and sunshine do their work on some musty ideas about sex, about women, and about men. It's amazing what a good housecleaning now and then can do for us. Don't be surprised if you feel better, more energetic, after reading this chapter.

Over the Hill?

I got a phone call one day from a young man who had seen me on a morning television show. He had tried calling while we were on the air, but the lines were busy. So the next morning he looked up my number and gave me a ring. His name was Pete.

"I'd like to check something out with you, Doc," he said, "if you've got a minute."

"Well," I replied, "to tell you the truth I'm in the middle of typing. But if it'll only take a minute . . ."

"Right," said Pete, "I'll make it quick, Doc."

Pete explained that he had been married to Patty, his childhood sweetheart, for four years. They had a two-year-old son. "You should see him, Doc. What a great kid!"

Pete and Patty were planning to have another child soon. Also, he told me, they were looking to buy a house. "Our first house, Doc. We're pretty nervous about it, you know?" He told me where they were looking, and how much he thought they could afford. He thought the prices they were asking were ridiculous. "But I figure it's never gonna get any cheaper, right, Doc?"

"Right," I said.

Then Pete started telling me about his job, and how he was looking to go back to college part-time. I interrupted him before he could finish. "What *was* that question you had, Pete?"

"Oh, yeah. Sorry, Doc. I guess I was sort of running on there. Well, anyway, getting back to me and Patty. The fact is that our marriage is pretty good. I mean, all things considered. I'm not saying it's perfect, but then show me the one that is, right?"

"Right," I replied. "So, *is* there a problem?" I was beginning to feel a little uptight. I'd quit typing halfway through a thought, and now it was gone, lost somewhere in Pete's househunting. I took a deep breath.

"I mean," Pete went on, "me and Patty, we get along. We have our fights. But who doesn't, right? And we've got a good baby. God bless him. Healthy as a bull. Eats like one, too. And I'm pulling in pretty good bucks, you know? But I do have this question, Doc, about sex."

I couldn't believe it. He was actually getting to the point! "Shoot," I said.

"Well, before we were married, me and Patty had sex maybe five, six times a week." He laughed. "Actually, Doc, I can remember one summer when we did it every day. The whole summer! Every day! Can you believe it?" He laughed. I tried to laugh, too.

"There were other times like that, too. But that was when we were a lot younger—you know what I mean?"

"Not exactly," I said, reaching over to turn my typewriter off. I had given in. I leaned back in my chair and put my feet up. "How old were you then, Pete, and how old are you now?"

"Now? I'm twenty-one, Doc. And Patty's twenty. Back then, though, when we were making it every day, I'm talking late teens. We've been going together since we were fourteen. Did I tell you that?"

"No," I said, "I don't think you did. That's interesting. But you still haven't told me what your question is."

Another laugh. "Oh, yeah! Sorry, Doc. Well, it has to do with how often we have sex."

"How often is that?" I asked.

There was a pause. "It varies, Doc, but I'd say it averages out to maybe two, three times a week."

"Sounds okay to me," I said. "Is there a problem with that?"

"Well, sort of. You see, my wife, Patty, she's a very sexual woman. Always has been. Actually, I think she's been even hornier since our boy was born. The problem is there are times when she wants it, but I don't. To tell you the truth, Doc, twice a week suits me just fine. Sometimes just once a week makes me happy. I'm just not up for it as much as I used to be. Which gets me to my question."

"Really?" I asked.

"What I wanted to know, Doc, was whether my not being so interested anymore is natural. Can you tell me? I mean, I'm too old to be wanting it every day, don't you think? Now that I'm getting a little older, I mean. I read somewhere that a man reaches his peak at eighteen, and that it's pretty much downhill from there. Is that true, Doc?"

I stiffened in my chair. Getting *older?!* Twenty-one years old, and he thinks *he's* over the hill?! Where did that leave me?!

Then, for a moment, I wondered if this was a joke. Was some

colleague playing a game? No, I decided, it wasn't that. Pete was real, and his question was serious. I told him he had nothing to worry about. "You're doing just fine," I said. "Don't worry about a thing." I told him that if he and Patty ever wanted to talk about it, I'd be glad to meet with them. I wished him luck with his househunting, then rung off.

It would be one thing if young Pete was a rare case. But he wasn't the first, nor was he the last man to ask me pretty much the same question: Am I over the hill, Doc? They ask me that whether they're twenty-one or sixty-one.

Pete's question brings home the fact that there is still as much fiction as fact out there when it comes to notions about sexuality. Despite sexual liberation, there are still an awful lot of myths that are passing for reality in our society. These are some of the cobwebs we need to clean out. To begin our housecleaning, let's follow up on Pete's question.

Sex and Ageing: Facts and Fictions

In a study conducted on a college campus, students were asked to estimate how often they thought their parents had sex. The results? The students, most of whom were between eighteen and twenty-two, consistently *underestimated* their parents' sex lives. In other words, their estimates about how often their parents made love were consistently *lower* than statistics from actual surveys of people their parents' age.

This study illustrates the bias we have about sex and ageing. There's a strong prejudice against older people being sexual, and this prejudice gets stronger the older you are. It isn't easy to feel okay about being sexual in the face of this antisexual attitude. I can remember one woman who came up to me after a lecture. She was about fifty-five, a social worker and the mother of three grown children. She told me that the main reason she and her husband didn't like the children visiting for more than a day was their antisexual attitudes. "You should see how uptight they are," she said. "They totally stifle our sex life! The way they act, you'd think it was against the law for my husband and me to kiss! They get embarrassed, and once or twice I've even gotten some comments. Well, let me tell you, I set them straight pretty quick!"

Is there sex after middle age? Probably the best source of hard facts to answer that question are some of the better surveys on sexual behaviour. The most famous (and in some ways still the best) are the surveys that were conducted by Alfred Kinsey and his associates in the 1940s. That research, and subsequent research, have all shown very clearly that sex doesn't drop out of people's lives as they get older. Men and women at forty, fifty, sixty, and older are sexually active.

More recent surveys show that men and women remain sexually active until either loneliness or illness get in the way. It's been found, for example, that from 50 to 70 percent of married men and women over the age of seventy say that they have an active sex life. In other words, most people, contrary to popular assumptions, stay sexually active so long as their health permits, and so long as they have a partner to make love with.

The most common causes for the loss of a sex life as you get older are failing health and widowhood. In stark contrast to the data on married men and women over seventy, among widowed people in this age group only 7 percent said they had any kind of active sex life. That's powerful evidence for the effects of loneliness and isolation that older people have to suffer.

Declining health is the other big culprit that can wreck the sex life of an older person. Some older people may not have a sex life, not just because they have gotten older, but because they are seriously ill. The data that they contribute to surveys, meanwhile, has the effect of bringing down the average for their age group as a whole. That's one way that we can underestimate the sex lives of older people: by looking at the ones who are ill, or who are alone.

Another study followed one group of men from their forties through their sixties. The results once again challenge the stereotypes. In one-third of this group, sex actually became *more* frequent as they got older. In another third there was no change in their sex lives as they went from their forties to their sixties. For those men who did report some decline, the main reasons (again) had to do with declining health and widowhood. So much for old ideas about sex and ageing!

Menopause and Climacteric: Myths and Facts

Menopause is another one of those areas, like the mysterious male "climacteric," that's been shrouded in myth and superstition. As a result, menopause has become something that many women dread. It's not an exaggeration to say that menopause has been cast as the beginning of the end of productive living— the start of a long downhill slide to the grave. It's been seen as the ending point of a woman's sexuality, and as the point where alienation begins to affect a marriage. No wonder a woman can get depressed or panicky at the mere prospect of approaching menopause!

None of the dreaded myths about menopause have been substantiated by hard evidence. Menopause can be a more (or less) uncomfortable time in a woman's life. On a physical level, the menopausal woman may experience uncomfortable shifts in body temperature, along with aches and pains. She may become more vulnerable to stress. Depending on how severe and long-lasting her physical symptoms are, a woman can also get depressed during menopause. She may be prone to getting irritable, and she may lose some of her interest in things, including sex. But that isn't part of menopause; it's a *reaction* to menopause. Specifically, it's a reaction to feeling physically uncomfortable. It's a reaction that anyone—man or woman—will naturally have when they're feeling out of sorts. Think of the last time you felt ill, even with such a minor thing as a cold. Did you feel sexy then? Could you have been a little depressed, irritable, and out of sorts? The same thing can happen in menopause. It's hardly unusual, and it usually passes once the physical turmoil of menopause settles down.

Some physicians and researchers have begun to look beyond the myths and superstitions, and their studies shed some light on the realities of menopause. They're finding, among other things, that many of the most uncomfortable physical symptoms can be relieved. There's even some hope that symptoms can be avoided, or at least minimized, through proper nutrition and exercise in the years before menopause.

Meanwhile, what about sexuality and menopause? Is it true that women typically lose interest in sex after the "change of life"? Is this some kind of biological fact of life that we just have to face, like it or not? No.

Research has shown that those women who pass through menopause and emerge with no interest in sex are by and large those women who had very little interest to begin with. They didn't enjoy sex very much *before* menopause. For many others, menopause leaves them with either no change, or an actual *increase* in sex drive. Why would a woman's interest in sex increase afterward? There are two big reasons. First, the children are usually out of the house by then, and a couple has time together for the first time in years. Second, being free of the worries of contraception can have a very liberating effect on a woman's sexuality.

Married women over sixty who say that they have no sex life usually place responsibility for this not on themselves but on their husbands. Usually they say it's poor health that's the problem, but sometimes they say that their husbands just aren't interested anymore. When they've been surveyed, the husbands usually *agree*. It seems, then, that men, as much as women, may be to blame if women don't have a sex life after fifty.

What about the notion of a male climacteric—the time in a man's life when he "naturally" loses interest in sex for physical reasons? By and large, it's pretty much the same story as for menopause. Men who don't take proper care of their nutrition, who work in high-stress jobs, and who don't stay physically fit, are naturally going to lose energy and stamina as they age. In almost every case it's this, and not some other physical change, that accounts for the "symptoms" of climacteric.

In men, the kind of dramatic hormonal changes that routinely occur in women during menopause just don't happen. The rate at which the body produces the hormone *testosterone*—which does play a role in sex drive in men *and* women—does seem to decrease as men (and women) age. However, the data we have so far is sketchy and incomplete. We don't know, for instance, how factors like nutrition, exercise, and effective management of stress relate to changing hormone levels. There's good evidence that factors like stress and poor physical conditioning relate to lower testosterone levels; so, what we may be seeing once again are figures that tell us about what happens to people who don't take care of themselves, or who don't know how to handle stress.

To maintain or to rebuild your own sex life after middle age, you may need to examine your own prejudices about *yourself*. What are your beliefs about sex and ageing? How does the information just related fit your own notions? Has your sexual relationship been a self-fulfilling prophecy, declining because you felt it *should* decline? If so, maybe you need to do a little house-cleaning.

Intimacy and Sexual Desire

"When I used to make love to Lynn, it was as if part of me was there, and part of me wasn't. Does that make any sense?"

I nodded. I'd heard these same sentiments before, from men and women, and Jonathan was expressing them well.

"I would be making love to her, but I wasn't feeling close to her. It's funny. On a physical level we were as close as two people can get, but emotionally we were on different planets. Looking back on it, it was very painful. I don't think she could have felt close to me, either. But neither of us ever talked about it. Eventually, we just stopped making love."

The idea that a couple can sustain a satisfying sex life over years without intimacy is a myth that comes mainly from our stereotypes about male sexuality. We stereotype men as intensely erotic, but as needing little *emotionally* in order to have a satisfying sex life. We think of men as being attracted to breasts, legs, and faces, full stop. We stereotype them as having little need for intimacy, affection, or tenderness in order to maintain their interest in sex. When a man loses interest, the first thing his partner usually thinks about is how she *looks*, instead of the quality of her relationship with him.

At the same time that we overestimate men's sexuality, we usually *under*estimate women's innate sexuality. We think of women as being turned on by men, and neglect their ability to strike their own sparks of sexual desire.

Obviously, both men and women can get turned on by appearances. That's simple enough to do, especially in the early phases of a relationship. Being "turned on" in this way, though, is very different from sustaining sexual desire in a relationship over a period of years. The less intimate we are, the harder it can be to strike those sexual sparks, and the more quickly they can die out. There's no doubt that a nice body can arouse sexual interest in the short run, but it's really surprising how quickly that initial attraction can wear off. Intimacy is what sustains our sexual interest over the long run.

The problem that lies at the heart of many sexually troubled relationships has to do with intimacy. Instead of being open and involved with each other, partners lead parallel lives, keeping large parts of themselves hidden. Instead of accepting each other as equals, they get entangled in conflicts over power and control. Instead of feeling connected, they feel alienated. Under these conditions sexual passion seldom lasts very long.

To begin understanding the role that intimacy plays in sex, let's talk about fears of intimacy.

Fears of Intimacy:
Are We Getting Too Close?

An exercise that I've found useful for getting people in touch with their feelings about intimacy is presented below. To begin, read each quotation: the one from Frederick Perls, and the one from Erich Fromm. Each of these men has been an influential psychotherapist and writer. Their ideas have influenced thousands of psychotherapists and perhaps millions of other readers. Interestingly enough, their ideas about relationships and intimacy, as summed up in the two quotations, could hardly be more different.

The deepest need of man is the need to overcome his separateness, to leave the prison of his aloneness. Man—of all ages and cultures—is confronted with the solution of one and the same question: the question of how to overcome separateness, how to achieve union, how to transcend one's own individual life and find at-one-ment.

—*Erich Fromm*

I do my thing, and you do your thing.

I am not in this world to live up to your expectations, and you are the not in this world to live up to mine.

You are you and I am I, and if by chance, we find each other, it's beautiful. If not, it can't be helped.

—*Frederick Perls*

After you have read the two passages, place a coin on the line beneath them, corresponding to where your own feelings lie. The more you feel sympathetic to what Perls's words say about relationships, the closer your coin should be to the Perls end of the line. On the other hand, the closer your feelings are to what Fromm is saying, the closer to his end of the line your coin should be. Don't think too much about this exercise; let your gut feelings be your guide.

Once you have some sense of where you feel most comfortable on the intimacy dimension, close your eyes and imagine yourself standing on that line, on your coin, somewhere between the two extremes. Let this fantasy sink in for a minute.

Now, imagine yourself moving, from wherever you are, toward Perls's end of the dimension; that is, from where you feel most comfortable toward his attitude about relationships. Again, focus on your gut feelings.

If you work at it for a while, you might notice that you begin to experience an emotional reaction to this little fantasy. The more you imagine yourself moving toward the Perls extreme, the stronger this reaction should be. Most likely, at some point you will start feeling a little uncomfortable. The closer you get to Perls's extreme, the more likely it is that you'll start to feel lonely or alienated. How lonely and alienated you'll feel depends on how close your original coin was to that end of the dimension. If your coin was close to the Perls view to begin with, then you probably won't feel that uncomfortable moving a little closer to it; but if your original placement was a lot closer to the Fromm side, then you'll probably feel very uncomfortable imagining what it's like at the other extreme.

See how far you can move in the Perls direction before you start feeling really uncomfortable. The farther you can go— meaning the more you personally identify with that point of view—the more likely it is that you're a person who prefers to be intimate with only a few, perhaps even just one other person. You gravitate toward relationships where you can maintain your personal space. You have major priorities in your life besides relationships. You don't like being put in a position of having to choose between a relationship and another significant priority, and at times you may be willing to sacrifice on the relationship. Your strong inclination is to resist demands being made on you by others. You like your freedom, and you don't feel comfortable with a lot of expectations from others. You admire self-sufficiency, and you dislike people who seem to be dependent on others.

❦ ❦ ❦

Return to your coin again. Let yourself relax for a moment. Take a couple of deep breaths. Now, close your eyes and imagine yourself standing on your coin again, but this time moving closer and closer to Fromm's end of the intimacy dimension. Let your imagination go and try thinking (and feeling) about what his idea of "at-onement" would be like. Imagine being that involved in a relationship.

Chances are that as you continue with this second part of the exercise, you'll eventually start to have another emotional reaction. Again, the intensity of your reaction will depend a lot on how close your original placement was to Fromm's ideas—on how sympathetic you naturally are to his philosophy. The feeling you get as you approach this other extreme, though, may also be uncomfortable. Instead of experiencing loneliness or alienation, however, it's more likely a feeling of being *smothered* or *trapped* that you'll have this time.

People who are most drawn to the Fromm philosophy of life are people who seek intense involvement. They like to be close with as many people as possible. They work hard to maintain relationships over time and distance. They much prefer being with people over being alone. They tend to have many expectations in relationships, and they believe deeply in commitment. In love, they seek relationships that become as intertwined as the tendrils of a vine. For them the image of love is an image of connectedness, of a permanent bonding of souls.

The anxieties that are aroused in this exercise have to do with *fears of intimacy*. There are two of these fears. The first is the fear of losing yourself—of losing your individuality or identity—in a relationship. It's a feeling of being trapped or swallowed up by another personality, that you're not an individual any more so much as an extension of someone else. Most people find this as aversive as alienation and loneliness.

The second fear is the fear of alienation, of being alone and unconnected in the world. In my experience with this exercise, most people avoid both extremes when first placing their coin on the intimacy dimension. They want to avoid both extremes: relationships where there is too little involvement and commitment, *and* relationships where there is so much involvement that they begin losing sight of themselves as individuals. In addition, most people who have done this exercise say that they move along the dimension from time to time, depending on their circumstances. There are times in their lives when they want more connectedness and involvement, and there are times when they want less. There are times when commitments seem right, and times when they may seem wrong.

Where are your own anxieties about intimacy? Are you more afraid of getting too involved, or of being alone? Have you changed over time? In what direction would you like to move?

Let's take a closer look at one particular fear of intimacy that's common today, which has to do with intimacy and individuality.

Does intimacy threaten individuality? Can it lead to a stifling dependency that robs us of our identity? Does it stand in the way of personal growth? Some people act as if they believed this was true. They say things like, "If I'm too open with my partner, I'll lose my privacy and my sense of individuality." Or they say, "If I were an open book, I'd lose my sense of who I am."

If you really think about these kinds of fears for a moment, they don't make much sense. Consider, for example, how many thoughts and feelings you have in a single day. Think of how many different experiences you have every day of your life. Now, think about how many of those thoughts and feelings, and how many of those experiences, you actually have time to share with someone. Even if you wanted to be an "open book," could you? Would you have enough time? Chances are you just don't have the time to share more than a small fraction of yourself with someone else, even someone you're very close to. Even couples who say they are intimate say that they need to be very selective in sharing, to make sure they can fit the important things into the time they have together. So, fearing that you can disclose too much of yourself seems irrational.

Fears of being too intimate usually cover up problems of trust or self-esteem, and often have to do with fears of being controlled or dominated in a relationship. The individual who doesn't trust, like the person who lacks self-esteem, will hesitate to open up for fear of losing control or being manipulated. They want to protect themselves, to maintain some sense of control—or at least self-protection—through secrecy. At times they can act like prisoners of war, giving only their name, rank, and serial number, even to their spouses! The idea of being intimate arouses anxiety and makes these people feel vulnerable.

Fears of opening up may be justified, or they may not be. Let me give you an example. Patty went to see a therapist after her boyfriend had walked out on her. As we got to talking about their relationship, I asked Patty to tell me what Harvey's complaints had been, and what had led up to his walking out.

"He just got sick and tired of my secretiveness," she replied.

"What secretiveness?" I asked.

Patty shifted in her chair. She looked uncomfortable and very guilty.

"Well," she said, "you see, I've always had this problem, only I've never really talked about it to anyone. Actually, it's only now—since Harvey—that I've begun to realize it *is* a problem."

"Being secretive, you mean?"

"Yes. I'd always thought of myself as independent, or private, but now I see that isn't what it is. I'm just plain secretive."

"How are you secretive?" I asked.

"It may sound funny, but what bothered Harvey the most— what really got him bent out of shape—was this thing I have about not wanting to tell him where I'm going when I go out. Well, it's actually worse than that. The truth is I sometimes lie about where I'm going. Even if I'm only going to the supermarket, if anyone asks me where I'm going I'll either say nothing or else make up a story."

"Do you get angry when Harvey asks you where you're going, or where you've been?"

"Yes."

"Why do you think you might want to protect yourself so

much, that you'd go to such extremes?" I asked. "Is it that you don't trust Harvey?"

"It's not that exactly. Or maybe it is. The thing is, I get this feeling that if I tell him where I'm going or who I'm with . . ."

"That he might want to control what you do, or who you see?"

"That's it!" exclaimed Patty. "That's what it feels like. Exactly. It's as though I believe that if I'm open, someone else will try to run my life."

"So the way to prevent being controlled is not to be open, even about little things like where you're going."

"Yes. It sounds crazy, doesn't it?"

"Not crazy, but defensive and guarded. I wonder, do you have a real need to be so defensive with Harvey? Is he the kind of person who really would try to control you, to dominate you?"

"That's what makes it seem crazy," replied Patty. "Harvey is the gentlest, most caring man I've ever met. I don't believe he wants to dominate me. In fact, I guess you could say that I'm the more dominant one in our relationship."

"And one of the ways you stay in the driver's seat," I suggested, "is by refusing to be open, or by lying about things."

Patty nodded. "Yes, I guess so," she said.

What Patty was doing, by keeping secrets and lying, was controlling her relationship with Harvey. By shutting Harvey out—by never discussing decisions with him before making them, by refusing to let him in on her plans—she effectively prevented him from having any say-so. This was how she'd always been in relationships. It was the only way she could be comfortable. The problem was, if she insisted on being this way, then she could only expect her relationships to lack feelings of intimacy. Ironically, though she was in control, it was her insecurity, her fear of being controlled, that motivated her to hold back.

Intimate relationships are relationships between equals. In these relationships power is *shared*. Sharing power in turn neces-

sitates an ongoing process of negotiation. It requires communication. Goals and priorities must be decided through dialogue,
and decisions reached through compromise and consensus. These
kinds of relationships have their conflicts, but they also have
their resolutions, along with a strong sense of connectedness and
involvement. There is a great deal of give and take, of getting
balanced with giving.

Take a few minutes to reflect on your relationship and particularly on your own and your partner's attitudes about power
and control. Use the following question as food for thought:

Consider how you and your partner handle things like finances,
major and minor decisions, priorities and plans. Would you say you
have a *corporate* relationship, where equality is based on being "separate but equal," or a more truly *egalitarian* relationship, where decisions and plans are made through negotiation and compromise?

PART II

Working on Love

Couples who want to keep the fires of passion alive and maintain intimacy over the long run need to share responsibility for achieving those goals. In order to be able to stay in love, they need to be willing to work on love. This means being willing to work alone, and together. They need to be able to look at themselves as individuals, and to think about what they each can do to help achieve their goals. They also need to be willing to look at what they can do together. ❧

5

Working Alone

There truly is magic to be discovered in relationships, if only you have the courage to pursue it. But if your attitude is to stand back and wait for the magic to find you, then you may be sorely disappointed. You can stand back, feel frustrated, and blame others, but the fact is that when it comes to not feeling close, or not feeling passionate, more often than not you're your own worst enemy.

Staying in love and overcoming problems of sexual desire and intimacy is a process of removing barriers. Ultimately, the fulfillment you've been looking for will be found when you are able to create and sustain a relationship based on shared power, openness, and mutual respect. Some of the barriers you may need to overcome are those that stand in the way of trust and self-esteem. Other barriers have to do with power struggles that stand in the way of equality between you. Finally, some barriers relate to priorities and commitments which compete for time and energy that's needed to build intimacy, to play, and to make love. Let's begin looking at these barriers, and how you can break them down.

In this chapter we'll look at some of the ways that you can work by yourself to liberate the passion inside you and open yourself to intimacy. In the next chapter we'll look at some of the ways that couples can begin working together, not only to enhance sexual desire, but to deepen the level of intimacy between them.

History Lessons

Individuals I've worked with have found it helpful to take some time to study their own histories from the point of view of intimacy and sexual desire. To do this, make a copy of the chart on page 75. The exercise involves these six simple steps:

Step 1: Select several different dates, starting when you were an adolescent, to your current age. Mark off all of these ages with small tick marks on the *time line.*

Step 2: Spend some time recalling what you were like at each of the ages you've ticked off. Remember what you looked like at each age, and what was going on in your life. Focus your thoughts especially on your sexuality at each of these stages in your life. Assign a *sexual interest rating* to each age on your chart. Your ratings can range from 0 (*minimum* interest in sex) to 100 (*maximum* interest in sex).

Step 3: After you've finished making ratings, connect them all to form a line. This is your *sexual interest history.*

Step 4: Think about the relationship you are now in. If you aren't in a relationship now, think about the last or longest one you had. Mark off the year when that relationship began on the time line. If it's ended, also mark off the year it ended.

Step 5: Spend some time remembering how you felt about your partner in this relationship at different points in time. Try to recall what your life, and what this relationship, was like at several times. In particular, think about how close or intimate you felt in this relationship at those times. Now, rate this relationship for intimacy for each of these times, from 0 (*minimum* intimacy) to 100 (*maximum* intimacy).

Step 6: When you're done, connect all of these last ratings to form a second line. This is your *intimacy history.*

Take a look at the two histories your work has created. Most people find that neither their sexual interest line nor their intimacy line is straight. Instead, they tend to be marked by peaks and valleys. Their sexual interest has not always been the same, and they have not always felt equally close to someone they were in a relationship with. If you think about it, this may seem obvious, but putting it all on a chart this way can lead to some interesting insights, and give you some ideas for action.

The peaks and valleys in your sexual interest, as well as in how intimate you've felt at different times, are related to different circumstances in your life at those times. For some people the sexual interest line reveals a general trend, either upward or downward. For some, growing up and getting older has meant a steady increase in sexual desire; for others, it has meant the opposite.

Think about the fluctuations in your own sexual interest history. What was your life like at times when your sexual interest was strong? Conversely, what was happening for you during those times when passion was less intense? Were you going through a difficult time personally? Were there problems in your relationship? What priorities were competing with your relationship for your time, energy, and attention? Were you feeling stressed, distracted, tired, or depressed at times when your sexual passion was at an ebb? How intimate would you say your relationship was when sexual passion was strong, and when it was weak?

Intimacy histories are usually highly correlated with sexual desire histories, particularly once you're an adult, and once a relationship has gotten past the honeymoon phase. In other words, most people who do this exercise discover that how they felt *sexually* was related to how *intimate* they felt at any particular point in time. When intimacy runs high, so usually does sexual desire; when intimacy ebbs, passion usually does, too.

Look again at the peaks in your intimacy history. What was your relationship like at those times? How much time did you and your partner spend together? What did you do together? Did you have fun, play, and relax together? Was anything else in your life as important as your relationship was when intimacy was strong?

Now, what about the low times—the valleys in your intimacy history? What was going on then? How were *you* spending your time, and how was your *partner* spending his or her time? Did you feel like you were a high priority in your partner's life? Was your partner a high priority in yours?

As you think back on it, what do you think accounted for the intimacy you may have felt at different times? What were you doing differently at times when you felt closer to your partner? What stops you from doing those things again now?

For a small minority of people, this history lesson is a painful one, for what they discover is that they've *never* felt intimate, *never* felt much sexual passion. These people need to look very closely at the role they've played in creating their own situation. Factors like low self-esteem and distrust can account for this pattern: for a life devoid of passion and intimacy. For now, let's stay with those people who may have known intimacy and passion at one time but who have found that it's more or less slipped out of their lives. These are people who have fallen out of love. This will be reflected in their charts by either a steady decline, or a sharp drop, in both lines. What accounts for this?

One of the most common culprits in problems of sexual desire and intimacy has to do with unresolved conflicts. Over time, issues that are avoided, rather than confronted and resolved, build up walls of anger that destroy love. They breed resentments that gnaw away at the foundation of a relationship. Meanwhile, distrust and alienation begin to breed. As alienation deepens, intimacy slips away. Intimacy and romance are among the first victims of this kind of creeping alienation, with sexual desire not far behind. When that happens, you've fallen out of love.

(Most)————→ 100

90

80

Desire/Intimacy   70
    Rating
60

50

40

30

20

10

(Least)————→   0 _____

(read vertically)

| 1 1 1 1 1 1 1 1 1 1 1 1 1 1 1 1 |
| 9 9 9 9 9 9 9 9 9 9 9 9 9 9 9 9 |
| 6 6 6 6 6 7 7 7 7 7 8 8 8 8 8 9 |
| 0 2 4 6 8 0 2 4 6 8 0 2 4 6 8 0 |

TIME LINE

Sometimes it happens that a couple will complain that one of them has lost their sexual desire, and that they definitely don't feel close any more, yet honestly feel that it isn't because one or both of them is sitting on some unresolved conflicts. In that case competing priorities—things that make intimacy and sex take a back seat in your life—may be a more relevant issue to look at.

Problems of sexual desire and intimacy are often associated with some kind of transition in a person's life that changes their priorities. Interestingly enough, it isn't necessarily only bad events that can trigger a loss of sexual desire or intimacy. I've known men and women whose relationships started to deteriorate after they had children—definitely not a bad event. Does that mean that children ruin marriages? No. But it does mean that you need to keep some perspective on your relationship after the children come. In the contemporary family, where there are typically two careers and children, too, it's easy to let priorities slip. It's dangerously easy to lose sight of the fact that relationships that get taken for granted usually deteriorate. Relationships need caring and attention just as much as children do. Without caring and attention, children and relationships stop growing.

Stress

Stress has become such a fact of life for most of us that we tend to ignore its presence and underestimate its effects. Many people today have jobs that demand a terrific amount of mental energy. At the end of the workday they come home not just tired, but drained. Realistically, before they can give anyone else attention or affection, they need to unwind.

What makes a bad situation worse for many people who find themselves caught in the "stress mill" is that their jobs involve a lot of responsibility that they can't seem to leave behind when they walk out the office door. Instead of breathing a sigh of relief and turning their attention to more pleasant things, they go home and worry about work. Under these circumstances they aren't good for anything much at all. By eight or nine in the evening, they're usually so burned out that the only thing they can do is fall asleep in front of the television.

Is it surprising that this kind of man or woman would complain of low sexual desire or a lack of intimacy in their life? Is it surprising that their spouse and children would feel neglected? Could you blame someone for feeling frustrated in a relationship with someone like this?

Though you would probably answer with a firm *no* to all of

the above questions, it's surprising how many people look at me as if I were crazy when I suggest that their jobs might be affecting their sex lives, or that their relationships might be suffering because of stress. Actually, it may not be the work itself that's responsible, so much as the way a person *handles* the stress it creates.

One man whose private life was suffering because of job stress and an inability to cope effectively with it was Bill. I suspected right off that this issue was going to come up, since he had to cancel our first two appointments because of last-minute business meetings. When he finally did show up, his first question was whether I had office hours on Sundays!

A typical workweek for Bill involved a minimum of fifty to a maximum of who-knew-how-many hours stretched over six or seven days. The pressures on him were intense. He had enormous responsibility and more deadlines that you could count. To make matters worse, he was one of those people who can't leave work at the office. He not only came home tired and tense, but preoccupied. In his mind he was still working. Though he was successful, he felt that his career was driving him, instead of him driving it. He found it almost impossible to relax, was irritable much of the time, and found his only escape in television.

What was the problem that brought Bill to therapy? His wife, he said, was depressed. Over time she was becoming more and more difficult to live with. The children, too, were becoming a problem. Their demands for attention seemed insatiable. They were becoming wild and rude. When he complained, his wife just got defensive and angry. She accused him of not loving her or of not caring about the children. He couldn't understand that. "Do you think my wife might be going through some kind of mid-life crisis?" he asked. "Could these be the signs of an early menopause?"

"I doubt it," I said, "since Amy is only thirty-two. I think there may be something else going on."

When I asked Bill if he thought his wife and children might be jealous of his job, he looked surprised. He couldn't imagine any reason for that. "Everything I'm doing is for them," he said. "I want them to have a good life. Why should they resent that?"

"I'll tell you why," I replied. "The fact is, Bill, that work has taken you away from Amy, and from the kids, too, for a long time. You're not only away from them physically because of your long hours, but when you're home it strikes me from what you say that you're not there emotionally. From their point of view, they've been jilted. They've lost a husband and a father to a job. They're probably feeling jealous and resentful. In their shoes you would, too."

Though his intentions may have been the best—Bill actually felt very committed to his family and his marriage—the fact was that somewhere along the way he'd lost his balance. Though he never intended it to happen, Bill had allowed the most fulfilling parts of his life—his marriage and his children—to take a back seat to his career. His marriage, his relationships with his children, even his physical health, were all showing the effects of unrelenting stress. Sex between him and Amy had all but disappeared. They never seemed to be able to be alone together without fighting. At thirty-four he already had the beginnings of a blood pressure problem. He had a nervous stomach that his doctor warned was slowly but surely working its way toward an ulcer.

The way out of this mess for Bill started with a personal reassessment. Together we spent some time trying to understand when and why he had lost his balance, and why he couldn't seem to keep work in perspective. This part of therapy—understanding *why* he was the way he was—was helpful, but the insights Bill and I reached were not, by themselves, enough to get him out of the hole he was in. We agreed, though, that unless he could find a way out, he was a good candidate for trouble ranging from a divorce to a heart attack. What Bill needed was *action*.

Bill started to reorder his life by sitting down and working out a schedule in which time with Amy, time with his children, and time for exercise were literally *written* in. You can do this for yourself. Just take a piece of paper and divide it into days and hours, like this:

DAYS

Hours	Monday	Tuesday	Wednesday	Thursday	Friday
6 A.M.					
7					
8					
9					
10					
11					
noon					
1 P.M.					
2					
3					
4					
5					
6					
7					
8					
9					
10					
11					
midnight					

To start, block out all the hours you're usually *sleeping*. Next, block out the hours you actually spend *at work*. For example, if you get to work at 9 A.M. and leave promptly at 5 P.M., Mondays to Fridays, block out all the hours between nine and five, Mondays to Fridays. But if you typically work longer, or on weekends, block out those hours, too. Next, block out all the time you spend *commuting* to and from work.

Now, before you block out any more hours, block out the following:

1. *Three* hours a week for personal exercise. These should be three separate hours, at least one day apart.
2. *Six* hours a week to spend, one-to-one, with your partner or spouse. You can spend this time any way you like. It can include activities ranging from talking to playing to going out. The one condition is that they must be six hours of one-to-one interaction.
3. If you have children, block out another *six* hours a week to be with them, either individually or with your spouse. These hours can be used for family activities, or for doing things one-to-one with your kids.
4. Block out *three* hours a week for personal fun. These hours can be used for anything from taking a walk by yourself, to locking yourself away with a good book, to just taking a nap.

Look at your chart now. How many hours are left? Whatever it is—no matter how much or how little—you can use it for anything you want. You can't, however, use the hours from midnight to 6 A.M., which were purposefully left off the chart, since these hours are needed for a minimum of sleep. If you mess with these, and consistently deprive yourself of sufficient sleep, you can guarantee that you'll feel stressed out *all* the time. (Note: If you work between midnight and 6 A.M., modify your chart and block off another six hours for sleep, as a minimum.)

Bill had a hard time with this exercise. For one thing, he didn't want to follow the rules. He wanted to negotiate the number of hours spent on exercise, his wife, and his kids. He didn't want to count commuting time. He argued with me, saying that exercise wasn't important. "I've got a career to take care of," he said.

"I understand that," I replied, "but you also have a body, and a marriage, and a family to take care of."

I pushed Bill toward making commitments to himself, his marriage, and his family. To his credit he hung in there, and after a while it started to work. He began to enjoy some of his playtime, and his time with Amy. Then his sex life started to improve. He found himself having fun again with his children and looking forward to weekends. As he saw that these changes in his personal life didn't lead to failure at work, he experienced a greater sense of control over his own life. He also felt a lot less stressed. Pretty soon he didn't need me any more.

Confronting Your Emotional Block

Many people who suffer from problems of sexual desire and intimacy have some form of emotional block. What does it mean to have an emotional block? Basically, it means that you are out of touch with what you feel. Usually it isn't just sexual passion that a person will be out of touch with, but other emotions as well. Some other feelings that emotionally blocked people commonly have a hard time with are anger and joy, anxiety and love, to mention a few. When you ask them what they're feeling, these people often won't be able to find a label for it. If they do know *what* they're feeling, they're apt to be at a loss to tell you *why*.

Why do people have emotional blocks? The most common reason has to do with feeling vulnerable. An emotional block is first and foremost a defence. Underlying it is anxiety about setting yourself on an emotional par with someone else, about revealing yourself and being open. What the emotionally blocked person is usually most afraid of is being taken advantage of. Hiding their feelings gives these people some sense of safety. Like many poker players, they believe that a straight face gives them an edge.

People who are emotionally blocked feel terribly vulnerable when their emotions get loose. They don't have much confidence in their ability to handle their own feelings, or trust that they won't be taken advantage of if their sensitivities are laid bare. The unspoken attitude of this kind of person is that if you stay in control of yourself, if you don't reveal yourself, others can't use or abuse you. So, they try not to show it when they're hurt, sad, or disappointed.

People with emotional blocks may be more closed to some emotions than others. They aren't necessarily out of touch with everything they feel. As a rule, however, people who try to control their feelings because they're afraid of being controlled are most guarded about those feelings that make them feel most vulnerable. These include feelings such as sadness and pain, discouragement and loneliness. It isn't hard to imagine what this kind of holding back means for intimacy in a relationship.

People can be so severely emotionally blocked that they actually believe (and can even convince others at times) that they have no feelings. If it's one particular emotion they're blocked on, then they might just convince themselves (and others) that they don't experience that one feeling. I've met people, for instance, who've told me that they've never been angry, and don't believe they're capable of it. It's as though anger didn't exist for them. I don't believe that. Despite what they say, I take their words as a sign of a severe emotional block, in this case with respect to anger.

Other people seem blocked not so much to anger as to sexual passion. It makes them feel vulnerable to reveal their sexual feelings. So they hold them back. They can do such a good job of holding back that eventually they convince themselves they have no sexual feelings to let go of.

In a society that encourages men, more so than women, to control emotions, it isn't surprising that emotional blocks are more common in men than women. Many of the men that I've seen for problems of sexual desire and intimacy are emotionally blocked in one way or another. They are afraid to reveal their emotions.

Ken decided to see a therapist after a big fight with his fiancée, in which she'd complained that he was cold and impossible to get close to. She found it frustrating, she said, that he seemed so reluctant to open up to her. These feelings had been building up inside her for a while, and she had to get them out, to see if marrying Ken was really the right thing for her.

This wasn't the first time Ken had heard things like that said of him. In the past he'd more or less shrugged it off; but this time, coming from a woman he loved very much and wanted very much to marry, it got to him.

Ken didn't exactly think of himself as cold, yet he had to admit that he was a pretty unemotional sort of guy. "I suppose I'm like my father in that respect," he said. "He's pretty controlled, the kind of father who puts you in awe. I can recall how he always criticized anyone who was emotional. I guess he didn't think very much of it."

Once Ken accepted that he came off as stonelike, he could understand how others could find him frustrating. But he didn't know how he could change that. Inside, he didn't feel cold. He wanted the same intimacy that his fiancée was looking for. But all he seemed able to offer was distance and cool self-control. To have the kind of relationship he wanted, I told him, he'd have to break the pattern set by his father.

Ken had learned so well to suppress all kinds of feelings— for fear of being ridiculed by his father—that he had no idea, most of the time, of *what* he was feeling. As embarrassing as it was to admit, he was often hard pressed to discriminate between feelings, to tell, for instance, whether he was feeling excited or anxious, sad or hurt. For him there were just two broad categories of "feelings": good and bad. Either he was feeling good, or he was feeling bad, full stop.

Aside from being out of touch with his feelings, Ken was anxious about letting them out. He wasn't confident that his emotions wouldn't embarrass him or lead him into trouble. These kinds of fears are extremely common in people with emotional blocks.

Some of the feelings Ken was most unsure of included fear, joy, sexual passion, and love. The idea of getting in touch with feelings like that, and of exposing them instead of keeping them inside, was scary. I told him he ought to give himself a lot of credit for having the courage to try it.

Ken learned to be more emotionally expressive, and so can you. It's one of the keys to intimacy and sexual desire. Passion is frequently on the list of emotions that people try too hard to control. At the same time, the guardedness of people who are emotionally blocked prevents them from being intimate.

As you think about yourself and your emotions, would you say that it's easy, or difficult, for you to express your feelings? How do you feel about people who are emotional? Are you drawn to people like that, or are you put off by their emotionality? Do you think you have a rich emotional life, or are you emotionally poor, like Ken?

Which of the following emotions do you think you might be inclined to overcontrol?

Anger	Sexual Desire
Sadness	Joy
Excitement	Anxiety
Fear	Shame
Pride	Guilt
Disappointment	Hurt

Are there other emotions, not included on this short list, that might be blocked for you? Can you discriminate among all of these emotions when you experience them?

Realizing that you have an emotional block is half the battle. The other half starts when you realize that no matter *why* you have this block, it's you and you alone who can remove it. Waiting for someone to come along who will recognize your hidden potential and bring out your emotional side may be a comforting fantasy. It's also a convenient way to avoid taking responsibility for yourself. Only you can change yourself. What you need to do is to reveal yourself, not wait for someone else to open you up.

You can start to open up by getting to know your emotional block. Chances are that you won't get very far if you simply try to pretend that your emotional block isn't there, when it is. A lot of people make their situations worse, and make it harder to change, simply by trying to ignore something that's a part of them. And that's what an emotional block is: it's a part of you. So you might as well get to know it.

You can get to know your emotional block by learning to catch yourself in the act of holding back your feelings. If you try paying attention to it, you can probably get in touch with your habit of self-control. You can learn to tell when you are holding a feeling back, instead of revealing it. Once you get that far, the next step is to learn to label the feeling you're holding back. Is it sadness or anger, pain or joy? Learning to identify your feelings is a skill. Like any skill it takes time, practice, and perseverance to develop. Don't give up too easily; you *can* do it.

Once you begin to get in touch with feelings, and understand what they are, you come to a critical choice point. One option is to do what you've been in the habit of doing, which is to hold back. Or, you can take a chance and express your feelings. That will make you feel vulnerable, but it will also open the door to new possibilities in your relationship. By doing that you'll be learning to live by your feelings, which is a rich man's life indeed.

Being emotionally blocked has one advantage—it minimizes your risks. It keeps you feeling safe and in control. Once you start getting in touch with feelings, and revealing them, you become more vulnerable than you were when you kept them hidden. You've set yourself on a par with someone else. They now know what makes you happy, or sad, or excited, or scared. On the other hand, you also become more accessible to that other person, and by sharing more of yourself, you can get closer to them. You've opened yourself to love.

Sexual Blocks

Certain people who are emotionally blocked claim that they aren't very sexual. From their point of view they just don't have much of a sex drive. The truth, though, is that these are people who are suppressing their sexuality. Sometimes they have it on such a tight rein that they really do lose touch with it. Their partners, though, usually sense the holding back on some level, and react to it as rejection. One woman I worked with confronted her husband on just this very point during one of our sessions. With a little support from me, she stuck to her guns and offered the opinion that, regardless of what her husband said, there were times when he was in the mood for sex.

"I can see it in your eyes," she said, and though he denied it I felt that she was probably right. She gave some examples of times when he seemed to start to respond to her sexual advances, but then caught himself and cut it short.

"Like the other night," she said, "I started caressing you, and you started getting turned on. Don't try to deny it, because I *know* you were. But then it was like you caught yourself, just like that, and something inside you clicked off. *You* clicked it off. I could tell when it happened. I could *feel* it."

This woman was in touch with her feelings. Her husband, though, wasn't in touch with his. He was actually one of the most emotionally blocked men I've ever met. He was charming, successful, and sharp as a tack, but so much concerned with control that he could never simply reveal his feelings. He was a great example of a man for whom holding back was a way of feeling in control. Attention and approval were things he gave out when he got what he wanted. Sex and affection were used very much in the same way. All of his emotions, from anger to love, were more or less tools in his hands. For many years this had worked for him. His wife, for example, could be counted on to react to his holding back by trying even harder to please him.

People who are emotionally blocked can come across to others—particularly people with low self-esteem—as powerful. To people who are inclined to feel inadequate, and who typically respond to criticism and rejection with guilt instead of anger, dealing with someone who holds back can be really difficult. In these kinds of relationships those with low self-esteem are the underdogs, always feeling that they aren't good enough. They believe that it's their inadequacies that are the problem in their relationship. So long as they believe this, they keep their partners from confronting the issue of their own emotional overcontrol.

Sexual blocks are overcome in the same way that you overcome any emotional block. You begin by accepting the fact that, like it or not, this is the way you are. Then you start to get in touch with sexual feelings, and approach them instead of running away from them.

The biggest step in overcoming a sexual block is the same step you need to take in overcoming any other emotional block, and that is to *share* your sexual feelings with someone else. You need to let them know when you're feeling sexy, turned on, interested. That will make you a little vulnerable, to be sure, but again it will open the door to new depths in a relationship.

Walls of Anger

A *wall of anger* is the name I use to describe the bitterness that can build up in an individual when resentments and anger go unexpressed in a relationship for a long time. Usually this happens when conflicts are avoided instead of confronted and resolved. Walls of anger destroy sexual desire and intimacy. Just as emotional blocks seem to me to be more common in men, walls of anger are more common in women. Why? Maybe it's because we raise women to be more docile and unaggressive than is good for them.

Walls of anger are born of frustration. When complaints go unheeded, when conflicts are not resolved through negotiation and compromise, they don't simply go away. Instead, they fester, and build up stores of resentment that end up coming between people. Of course, you don't have to be a woman to build a wall of anger. In many ways, unassertive men find themselves in this same situation. They, too, can fall out of love for this reason. I worked for a time with a man for whom sexual desire and intimacy were blocked by a wall of anger.

"Patty can really lay me low," Bert said, "She can be loving - a wonderful person, really - but if I do something wrong, let her down or disappoint her in some little way, she can make me feel like I'm lower than a snake. My mother was that way, too."

Bert was carrying around a lot of unexpressed resentment, not only because of the way his wife criticized him, but because he felt relatively powerless in his relationship with her. He found it hard to fight, to confront her on issues, or to persist in trying to get what he wanted. He lacked confidence in himself, and he felt that in confrontations he always ended up losing. "I can start out feeling right, but I always end up feeling wrong," he complained.

"It's hard to feel sexually attracted to someone or to want to get close to them when you feel that way, isn't it?" I asked.

Bert nodded. Until he was able to confront his wife more effectively, I said, which meant believing in himself more, and feeling less intimidated by her judgmental and self-righteous attitude, there was no way he was going to want to make love to her or open up to her. Until then, there'd be little honesty, play, intimacy, or sex between them.

I believe that most—maybe even all—men and women who lose their sexual desire, or whose relationships lack intimacy, need to look for a wall of anger. What these people have in common is frustration and disappointment, sometimes years of it. Sometimes sex itself may be one of the causes of that resentment. Maybe it hasn't been loving enough, fun enough, or caring enough. Maybe it's been a one-way street: a lot of giving, and not much getting.

In other cases, a sexual relationship may be less the cause than the victim of a wall of anger. Maybe, as in Bert's case, it's other things that cause the resentment, and sexual desire gets lost in it.

Once you've found your wall of anger, examine it closely. What's it made of? What purpose does it serve? Is it worth the price you pay to keep it there? Does it get you what you want?

Losing interest in sex, like withdrawing affection in general, can be an indirect way of getting back at someone. Ask anyone who's been on the receiving end of this ploy; they'll testify that the old cold-shoulder treatment can be an effective punishment. Especially when it's wrapped in a thin veil of excuses, sexual rejection can really get to you.

Could some desire to get even lie behind a wall of anger that's poisoning your relationship? Who wants to get even, and why? Could there be other ways to settle the score, or resolve the conflict?

Holding out on sex can also be one way of exerting power in a relationship. The problem with it, though, is that it's *negative* power. It's a desperate effort at best, usually the last resort of a person who feels powerless otherwise. It involves self-denial, and it hurts your self-respect to use sex in this way.

Do you ever suspect that your partner uses sex in an effort to get something from you? Do you ever use sex this way? How else could you try to get what you want?

Sexual withdrawal, last of all, can be a crude way of establishing some balance of power in a relationship. Again, though, this is a desperate effort, requiring self-denial as the price of equality. It creates something more akin to a standoff than real equality based on mutual respect.

A healthy sex life is an expensive price to pay for establishing some equality, for getting what you want, or for getting even. There *are* better ways to do all of these things. If you've gotten turned off to sex, or feel alienated from your partner, only some honest soul-searching on your part will reveal what role any of these hidden motives may play in it.

To recapture intimacy and passion, people who've retreated behind walls of anger need to come out into the open. They need to express their feelings directly, instead of keeping them hidden. If it's revenge they're after, they need to say clearly what it is they feel betrayed over or angry about. If they want something, they need to try to get it through confrontation, negotiation, and compromise, not through manipulation. How much of this applies to your relationship, and to you as an individual?

❦ ❦ ❦

As you can see, walls of anger aren't torn down without some negative feelings being let loose in the process. This may be an unpleasant prospect, but the potential rewards are great. If you have the courage to venture down that road, remember this, and take heart from it: Relationships that are closed to negative feelings, to conflict, and to confrontation, sooner or later become closed to positive feelings and to intimacy and passion as well. When bad feelings are held back, for whatever reason, good feelings, instead of being brought out into the open, eventually start getting held back, too. Individuals who say to me that they never get angry, like couples who tell me they never fight, often turn out to be unhappy. Their relationships are lacking in warmth, closeness, fun, or passion. Outwardly they may appear serene, but inwardly they're alienated.

If you've been feeling turned off from your partner, whether it's been for a few weeks or many years, you ought to think about confronting the wall of anger you've probably built during that time. Ask yourself the following questions:

- Are there things that make you angry, past or present, that you haven't talked to your partner about?
- Do you have complaints about your sexual relationship that you haven't expressed?
- Do you feel that your partner doesn't take you seriously, or won't compromise or negotiate with you?
- Are you afraid of conflict?
- In general, are you open in expressing angry feelings and confronting your partner, or do you hold back these feelings a lot?
- Have you given up on trying to get what you want from your sex life? From your relationship in general?
- Do you sense that you hold back, either sexually or with your affection, as a way of getting even?

Just as people who are emotionally blocked sometimes cop out by waiting for someone to come along and free them, so do people with walls of anger have their favorite excuses for not doing something about it. The one that I've heard most often goes something like this: "Why should *I* have to get angry? Why can't my *partner* learn to be more considerate?" A slightly different version of basically the same excuse goes like this: "How come I have to *ask* for everything? Why doesn't my partner know me well enough, or care enough, to give me what I want?"

Of course it's reasonable to expect consideration from someone who's supposed to love you. Naturally you would also expect this person to want to please you. But does that mean that you should never have to speak up, never have to ask for something, never have to stand up for yourself, or never have to fight? Can you reasonably expect someone else to be able to read your mind, or to give you what you want without ever having to be asked? Can everything always come easily, without a word of conflict? Is it reasonable to expect that a relationship can work over the long run without confrontations, and without negotiation or compromise?

A relationship takes more than good intentions if it's to last and be good. It needs communication, it needs compromise, and it needs ways of getting conflicts out into the open. The best reason for getting angry and facing up to conflicts is that when relationships are open to these things they go beyond the level of fairy-tale romances. When they're open to confrontation and compromise, they become real.

Walls of anger, if they've been there long enough, make a person bitter and emotionally numb. Depending on how bitter and numb you might be feeling, the longer the "thawing out" phase in intimacy-building can take. You may need to persevere, but the end results will make it worth your while. As a guideline, follow these simple rules:

Rule 1: Know what you want from your partner.
Rule 2: Let your partner know what you want.

Rule 3: PERSIST. Try to get what you want.

Rule 4: COMPROMISE, but don't simply give up.

Rule 5: EXPRESS your frustration, anger, or whatever it is you feel if your partner ignores your needs.

Rule 6: Expect the same from your partner.

6

Working Together

Chapter 5 addressed some of the things you can do as an individual to understand problems of intimacy and sexual desire better and learn what you can do about them. Being able to look at yourself, and more importantly being willing to change, is essential if you hope to be in one of those rare relationships that is able to stay together *and* stay in love.

Much of the work involved in staying in love is work that a couple needs to do together. Invariably, one of the things that divorced couples say, looking back, is that they were never able to work well together. They had problems compromising, setting shared goals, and communicating with each other. Issues were avoided rather than confronted, and alienation replaced involvement. There was no true sense of equality and mutual respect; instead, there were constant struggles over power and control. This chapter will give you some ideas about how to overcome these patterns. We begin where we left off, by looking at the vital importance of facing up to conflicts.

Love and the "Corporate" Marriage

Relationships that are big on personal space can be short on shared space. They can be relationships in name but not in substance. In these situations partners may lead parallel lives that touch each other all too little. These *corporate* relationships may work, but they work (and feel) more like corporations than marriages. In these relationships there's more of an emphasis on separation than there is on togetherness. There may be equality, but it's based on disengagement more than on negotiation. There can be surprisingly little trust in these relationships. Each partner may feel free to pursue their own goals, but there's a shortage of shared goals. There is little sympathy for or interest in compromise, much less sacrifice, in a corporate marriage. The emphasis is on individuality and personal growth here, so strongly that it leaves little room for the relationship to emerge or grow as a "third partner."

Corporate marriages may seem calm on the surface. That's because one of the spoken or unspoken rules in corporate marriages is that partners don't fight. But relationships that seem calm on the surface can be very troubled below that surface. When a couple tells me they never fight, or when an individual says they never get mad, I feel uneasy. I wonder what that means. I'm suspicious because one thing I've learned is that relationships without conflict can also be relationships without intimacy, and that where there's no fighting, there also may be no sharing.

Couples who tell me they seldom disagree or fight can also complain that they don't feel close. Their sex lives may not be what they'd like them to be. They don't make love as often as at least one of them would like to, and when they do make love it doesn't make them feel close or connected to each other. Barbara and Dan had these kinds of complaints. Their marriage was barely a year old, yet already they both were feeling that something vital was missing.

Both successful young professionals, Dan and Barbara were two attractive, active people who'd been drawn together on the basis of shared interests and values. One of those values, it turned out, was a strong belief in "personal space." They believed in giving each other as much freedom as possible, to pursue their careers, their own goals, their individual interests. They believed in asking for compromise as little as possible, and in expecting sacrifice not at all.

On the surface, it was one of those relationships that had everything going for it; on the surface, all was calm and right. Privately, though, Dan admitted that he had already started asking women out to lunch. Barb, too, said that she had noticed her eyes starting to wander. These were bad signs, obviously. I felt sad for this young couple, who I sensed still had a lot of feeling for each other, but who were already falling out of love.

Aside from their interests and values, Barbara and Dan had something else in common, something that wasn't so much of an asset to their relationship. They both came from families where conflicts were typically avoided and buried, instead of being confronted and resolved. Disagreements were swept under the carpet, rather than brought out into the open. Little was revealed in the way of emotion, especially negative emotions like anger.

Like most couples, Dan and Barbara had made no connection between their family backgrounds (or the styles of dealing with conflict that their backgrounds had influenced) and their later beliefs and attitudes, including their belief in personal space, their attitudes toward confrontation and compromise, and their fears of anger. Lacking insight into the role their personal histories played in their own problems, they felt lost. Each was more or less aware of the way their parents had been, and neither liked it much; but neither of them could see the link between that and the problems they were having as a couple.

As I got to know them better it became very apparent to me that Barb and Dan, like their parents before them, avoided showing emotion, especially negative emotions. They avoided conflict and confrontation, too. They tried to justify all of this in the name of personal space and freedom. When I brought this idea up, they defended themselves. Maybe I thought they were avoiding things, but from their point of view it was just mutual respect that was motivating them.

I figure that even the most patient and understanding people are bound to have conflicts, and that's why I'm immediately suspicious when a couple tells me they don't fight. Since I have yet to meet two people who agree on everything, who always want exactly the same thing at the same time, I expect that any reasonable couple should have their fair share of conflicts. Dan and Barb, though, told me that they hadn't had a single fight in all the time they had been together. That didn't make sense to me, and I told them so. Either they were two saints who just happened to meet and fall in love or else they *had* to be avoiding something. Dan admitted I had a point there. Then Barbara spoke up. Maybe there were some hidden and unresolved issues between them, she said. My ears perked up. I was willing to bet, I said, that one or both of them was holding on to some resentment, and that it was slowly but surely coming between them.

That is exactly what was happening. And because they couldn't express *bad* feelings, like anger, and confront each other on issues, Dan and Barbara were beginning to hold back on the *good* feelings they had for each other. A big part of our work together was helping them see the connection between avoiding conflict and avoiding intimacy.

In effect, not only intimacy, but sexual desire, was the price that Dan and Barb were paying for avoiding conflicts. It's a pattern I've seen many times, and when I see it I worry for the couple that's caught up in it. I know that as long as they won't confront each other, they won't feel close, and that if they don't feel close they won't feel turned on, either.

Unresolved conflicts and unexpressed anger won't simply go away if they're ignored. They simmer below the surface of a relationship, and slowly eat away at it. Intimacy and passion fall victim to resentments that fester.

For me, the most important measure of the potential of a relationship to last and be fulfilling isn't whether it's open to positive feelings, but whether it's open to positive *and* negative feelings. Certainly the positive things—the love and caring, support and affection—need to be there. There also needs to be a willingness, though, to accept and work through the negative. To really grow, a relationship needs to be open to anger as well as to love, to sadness as well as to joy. The longer the list is of things that partners feel they *can't* say to each other, or of emotions they feel they *can't* express, the less potential there is for love—for intimacy and passion—to thrive over the long run.

For Barbara and Dan the problem started when she began to feel that he didn't want to listen to her when she had anything bad to say. "As long as I'm emotionally up," she said, "everything is fine. But as soon as I'm feeling depressed, or angry, or hurt, I feel that Dan doesn't want to hear it. He turns me right off."

"How does he do that?" I asked.

"By changing the subject. Or by humoring me in a way that makes me feel he doesn't take me seriously. Or sometimes he just ups and leaves the room, walks out on me while I'm in the middle of talking to him."

At first, Barbara said, she felt guilty, as though there was something wrong with not feeling up all the time. The idea of keeping bad feelings to herself played into one of her "ideals" about relationships: that partners shouldn't burden each other with their personal problems. Somehow she thought this would make a relationship better. But if a relationship, especially a marriage, isn't for being open, then what's it for? If Barbara kept quiet about anything that was bothering her, I said, sooner or later I'd expect her to start feeling resentful, and eventually to feel alienated from Dan.

That's what was happening, Barbara said. At the same time that she was feeling more distant from Dan, she was beginning to lose interest in making love with him.

Barbara noticed that Dan did the same thing with his own negative emotions as he did with hers: he avoided them. Whenever something happened that seemed to make him mad, he denied he was angry. When he looked obviously unhappy, he said it wasn't true. She noticed that he never fought; instead he tried to make light of something, or joke or distract his way out of a potential argument.

As Barbara withdrew some of her affection from Dan, she triggered a vicious cycle that led the two of them down the path to alienation. As he finally admitted—just before things started getting better—Dan felt hurt and rejected by his wife's withdrawal. But instead of saying so, he did what he usually did, which was to avoid it. Then he, too, started to withdraw and build his own resentments.

Exactly *what* Dan and Barbara disagreed about doesn't matter. The content of the issues in their marriage is not important. What is important is the fact that they were *avoiding* each other, and that this avoidance was creating alienation.

The healing process, for Dan and Barbara and for other couples, is a process of breaking down walls and opening up a relationship to the bad as well as the good. As they begin to be more open with their negative feelings, to learn how to fight and to compromise, Dan and Barb and many others have told me that they start feeling closer again. "I can't believe it," Dan said in one of our later sessions. "Last week we had two arguments, but we also made love twice, and it was great!"

Avoiders and Confronters

Some people avoid conflicts simply because they don't have confidence in their ability to stand up for themselves and strike a reasonable compromise. These people need to learn how to fight better. Then there are those people who are so insecure that they can't stand to compromise. For them, a compromise feels like a horrible personal loss. These people are poor listeners and tend to be rigid and judgmental. Finally, there are people who turn away from problems because they feel their responsibility goes beyond merely confronting them. They feel responsible for solving problems all by themselves.

Dan more or less fit into this last category. These men and women take on others' problems as their own. They feel burdened by others' worries. They feel pressured to solve problems single-handedly and make everyone happy. No wonder they end up being avoiders!

In his own family, Dan's mother had played helpless a lot. Instead of dealing with them herself, she'd bring her worries and frustrations to him. Starting at an early age he had adopted the attitude that it was his responsibility to solve these problems and make his mother happy. He tried his best. He listened to her complaints. He gave her his best advice. But it never seemed to work. The same problems came up again and again. Nothing ever got better.

What did Dan's wife complain about? You guessed it: that Dan didn't want to hear about problems! What lay at the core of his resistance to dealing with issues in his marriage were his earlier experiences with his mother. The unconscious lesson from those years had been that others' problems could not be solved. No matter how sympathetic he was, he believed, no matter how many helpful suggestions he might make, his expectation was that things would never improve. The same complaints and conflicts would always be there, and he would always feel guilty for not being able to solve them.

Together, Dan and I decided that his mother's problems weren't really meant to be solved. Most likely, talking to him was a form of emotional release for her. As a child and teenager, though, Dan lacked the maturity to see it in this perspective. Like most youngsters, he took things at face value and missed the point. He fell into the trap of trying to solve unsolvable problems. Burning out on this caused him to develop the unsympathetic attitude that his wife later found so annoying.

Are you an *avoider*, or a *confronter*? If you're an avoider, which of the following situations describes you best? Why are you motivated to avoid issues or confrontations?

• Because I lack confidence in my ability to negotiate a compromise successfully.

- Because the idea of compromising about anything is distasteful to me.
- Because I feel that someone else's complaint becomes my problem to solve.

Relationships that are open—where sharing isn't limited to good feelings only—tend to be a lot more intense than relationships that are closed to conflict, and where the word *negotiation* isn't in the vocabulary. The mutual involvement in issues in these relationships deepens their level of intimacy, just as much as affection and support do.

To recapture intimacy, you need to determine *if* you (or your partner) is an avoider. Then you need to ask yourselves, *why* do you avoid? Last, and most important, you need to learn to become confronters, for the sake of your relationship as much as for your own good as individuals.

Rules for Fair Fighting

The last chapter ended with a set of rules you could follow when trying to learn to express your feelings instead of keeping them in. Extending these rules to your relationship and trying to follow them *together* can open the way to a more intimate, involving, and intense relationship. Make no mistake about it: fighting well together can pave the way to making love together.

Keep these rules in mind. Better yet, copy them down and tape them to your refrigerator door, your bathroom mirror, or a place where both of you will see them every day. Following these simple rules will change you from an avoider to a confronter.

Rule 1: Remember that avoiding conflicts will only make you withdraw from each other. To get closer, confront your problems.
Rule 2: Keeping bad feelings in leads to keeping good feelings in. Share *all* your feelings, if you want to keep love alive.

Rule 3: Learn to negotiate with each other, by hearing each other out, to understand what the other person wants.

Rule 4: Experiment with compromise: with giving in order to get.

Priorities Versus Commitments

Priorities are to commitments what words are to actions, as the following exercise shows. Use it to assess your relationship and set goals. You can do it alone, and use it as more food for thought. For even better results, do it with your partner. You might want to work on it separately, and then compare your responses.

Under the Priorities and Commitments heading that follows, you will find a list of various things that a person can value. People differ in how important these different things are to them. As you go through the list, think about how important each item on it is to you personally. Then, go through the list and rank all of the items, from the one that is *most important* (#1), to the one that is *least important* (#10). Put these rankings in the "Priority" column.

Priorities and Commitments

ITEM	PRIORITY	COMMITMENT
Privacy	# _____	_____ %
Health/Fitness	# _____	_____ %
Sex	# _____	_____ %
Career/Work	# _____	_____ %
Children/Family	# _____	_____ %
Recreation	# _____	_____ %
Friendships	# _____	_____ %
Intimacy	# _____	_____ %
Housekeeping	# _____	_____ %
Hobbies	# _____	_____ %
		100%

101

After you've carefully ranked your personal priorities, think about how much time you actually spend on each of them. Imagine that all your waking time, added together, would total 100 percent. Divide this 100 percent among the ten priorities, so that when you add up the percentages given to each area, the total of the scores in the "Commitment" column comes to 100 percent. The more time you actually devote to any one thing, like housekeeping or work, the higher the percentage for that item should be. This second part of the exercise might take some time, but when you combine it with the first part it will add a great deal to the overall usefulness of this exercise.

Now, compare your priorities to your commitments. Your *priorities*, of course, are the things you say are most important to you. They are your "words." Your *commitments*, on the other hand, have to do with the way you actually spend your time. They're your "actions." How closely do they match your words?

In an ideal world, commitments and priorities would match. In actuality, probably very few of us could make that claim. Like many people I know, I enjoy my career, but I honestly think I spend more time at it than I would ideally like to. I enjoy working around the house, too, but then there are times when cooking and fixing are all I seem to do. I often feel that I have to squeeze recreation and friendships into the cracks in my life, and my desire to be with my wife or family sometimes competes with my need for quiet time alone. And so on. Nearly everyone I know has similar kinds of feelings about their priorities versus their commitments.

How about you? How do your priorities stack up against your commitments? Where are you spending the biggest chunks of time? Are these the things that are most important to you?

If you are in a relationship, how do your priorities compare to your partner's?

Many couples who fall out of love get tangled up in conflicts of priorities versus commitments. As you look through the preceding list you can see how some of the priorities listed there fit neatly into concepts like "personal space" or "personal growth." These are priorities that people can easily pursue on their own. Other items on the list, however, are priorities that center around relationships. They have more to do with intimacy and involvement. Fulfilling these priorities means putting more time into doing things together.

Shared space is another way to think about intimacy. In general, more intimate relationships have more shared space. In less intimate relationships the "space"—in other words, priorities and commitments—is mainly divided up between "his and hers," or "mine and yours." In these relationships there may be very little that's "ours." Let me give you an example.

When they did this exercise, Marge and Jake came up with very different answers. Her top three priorities were intimacy, sex, and family; his were career, recreation, and privacy. Between his top two priorities alone, better than 80 percent of Jake's waking hours were committed. When time alone was added in, that figure increased to 95 percent. Obviously, that left little time for anything else. He had little time to commit to other priorities, and the quality of his marriage reflected this.

Their differences in terms of priorities and commitments also reflected Marge and Jake's different backgrounds. He came from an achieving but emotionally distant and competitive family, and grew up to be competitive and emotionally controlled. He approached work and play with the same aggressiveness, and didn't really enjoy anything that didn't have a competitive edge to it. He resented being asked to change his priorities, and rejected the notion that you have to sacrifice or compromise in order to have a good marriage. In his family, a man's work always came first. He wanted Marge and the kids to be understanding when he worked six days a week, when he'd spend spring weekends fishing with friends instead of camping with them, or when he'd rather listen to music alone than play a game with them.

Marge had grown up in a large family. They had little money but were very close and tended to pull together a lot. What she wanted most in life—the things she'd looked forward to from the time she was a young girl—were a happy marriage, a house, and children. She had a great deal of admiration for Jake's ambition and success, but she felt locked out of his life by all the things he did that didn't have to do with her or their children.

When they first came to therapy Jake's complaint was that Marge didn't want to have sex. That was true enough. She had withdrawn her affection, but it seemed clear that she did this because her marriage was lacking in the intimacy she needed in order to feel sexual desire. For her, like most people, intimacy was a *condition* for sexual desire, and she knew it. She knew that she needed to feel involved and connected before she could feel sexually passionate. She needed time together, and she needed communication. Under those conditions—which had been there earlier in her relationship with Jake—she had an intense interest in sex. Without them, her sexual desire quickly faded.

Although Jake was the one who was complaining about not having enough sex, his own sex drive was not nearly as strong as Marge's was when she was getting the intimacy she needed. He would have been content to make love once every couple of weeks, but ideally she would have liked it a lot more often than that. As it was, she wasn't initiating sex at all anymore, and Jake was getting turned down almost every time he did. On the surface, that made it look, at first, as if he was the one with the sex drive, while she was the one with the problem.

Who really had the "problem" in this relationship? You could say that they both did. But that's not so important. The solution to Jake and Marge's difficulties had very little to do with finding fault and laying blame. It had a lot to do with understanding the conflicts in priorities and commitments that lay beneath the problem. Once this was clearer to both of them, they had an opportunity to solve their dilemma through negotiation and compromise. Their goal was to make a commitment to love, and their challenge was to build shared space. They were able to do this by establishing shared priorities that were matched by real commitments.

When people talk about wanting personal space, what they usually mean is that they want to be able to reserve time for activities outside of their relationship. They want to be respected for having priorities like a career, a hobby, or friendships. That's easy enough to understand. At the same time, you must recognize the fact that you can't have intimacy if you don't make a commitment to it. A good sex life depends on there being enough shared space as well as personal space in your life. If there's too much *me-ness*, and not enough *we-ness*, then love will suffer.

Making a Commitment to Love

Looking through your list of priorities, where does *intimacy* fit in? How high is it on each of your lists? Can you agree on how much of a priority it should be?

Think about the kinds of things you used to do that made you feel intimate. How much time do you spend doing these things now? In other words, how much of a *commitment* have you made to intimacy?

If you want intimacy and a good sex life, what has to happen to some of your other priorities? Which commitments are you willing to reduce, in order to have a better relationship?

Encouraging Change

Common sense tells us that before a couple can begin the work of rebuilding a damaged relationship they need to spend some time settling old business and healing wounds; in other words, they need to clear the air. Trying to ignore alienation that's been festering for years simply doesn't work. Resentments that are rooted in years of frustration will not conveniently disappear just because we've decided to turn over a new leaf. Unfortunately this is often what one or both partners secretly hope will happen. I have the unhappy task of telling them that this won't work, that they won't be able to bury old issues until those issues have seen the light of day.

The process of laying bare unresolved anger and pain can be difficult, but it's a critical step in the healing process for couples who want to rebuild love. Once a couple has had a chance to do this—to air old gripes and hear each other out—they must make a critical decision: Will they hold on to old resentments, or are they willing to let them go long enough to recognize and encourage each other's efforts to change?

Sharon and Michael both came from backgrounds that weren't conducive to letting go of grudges. My impression of his family was that it was a household devoid of warmth, where criticism masqueraded as sympathy, and rejection as support. Sharon found it difficult to be around Michael's family. Within hours she'd find herself starting to feel irritable and depressed. When she first met them she was struck by how different Mike seemed from them; but after a while she began to think differently, and to see the ways in which he'd been cut from the same cloth.

Mike was like his parents in that it was all but impossible for him to offer encouragement and sympathy without it coming out sounding like criticism and rejection. The longer she was with him, the more painful and frustrating Sharon found it to talk to Mike about things that were bothering her. It was even worse when it came to conflicts. He seemed impossibly defensive and would fly off the handle in response to the most minor complaints. She felt that she couldn't express the least bit of anger or dissatisfaction for fear of being subjected to a vicious counterattack. What made matters worse was that some of Sharon's complaints had to do with their sex life. In truth, she found Mike more or less stiff and mechanical in bed. He was too quick to reach for her genitals, too eager to move from foreplay to intercourse, and too ready to fall asleep after orgasm. She kept her feelings to herself for the first year or so of their marriage, thinking that maybe the problem was in her. Maybe she wasn't responsive enough, she thought. Maybe she needed to loosen up more. Maybe they needed more diversity. Maybe this; maybe that. So she tried doing different things, tried taking different attitudes, but nothing changed.

Sharon kept her feelings in because she was afraid that Mike's reactions to being criticized would be all the worse if the criticism was about his sexuality. When it got to the point of either speaking up or turning off to sex, though, she finally told him how she was feeling. Mike's reaction was bad. He attacked, saying it was Sharon who had the problem. She avoided the issue after that.

Three years passed, and Sharon built up so much resentment that her sexual desire became completely blocked off. She didn't feel close to Mike any more, and privately she wondered whether she even loved him. When we met, she honestly believed that she had no sexual desire at all. She hadn't made love with Mike for over a year and a half. The very idea of it made her more or less sick. She was of the opinion that men's bodies were ugly, and that she was incapable of a sexual response.

I told Sharon that her sexual desire was probably not so much nonexistent as buried beneath a pile of resentment. I also suggested that she'd played a role in the downward spiral that her marriage and sex life had taken. She didn't like my saying that, but she was willing to hear me out.

Judging from the way she described them, Sharon's family struck me as not nearly so harshly rejecting as Mike's, but it didn't seem to me as if it were exactly overflowing with approval, either. It was a picky kind of family. As a result, Sharon grew up being thin-skinned and defensive, very much like Mike but less extreme. In dealing with her family, and in particular with a brother who had teased her constantly while they were growing up, the only strategy she knew was holding back. She would clam up and withdraw. She was a master at the cold shoulder, and this would be her revenge. She was an avoider, not a confronter, and that's what contributed to the problems she had with Mike: rather than standing up and fighting, she gave up and withdrew.

In order for things to be able to get better, and more importantly to stay better, Sharon and Mike both needed to become effective confronters. She had to learn to approach life more aggressively, to stand up and fight. He needed to learn to listen, and to view compromise as a solution to problems, instead of seeing it as a personal loss.

Sharon had a hard time letting go of her resentments. She held on to them so tenaciously that she very nearly sabotaged any chance for improving her marriage. Even after he'd owned up to some of his problems and genuinely wanted to change, Mike got nothing but discouragement from her. When he reached out—tried to compromise or give her what she wanted—her reaction was basically, "That's not good enough."

Left alone, I was sure that Sharon would soon discourage Mike, who after all wasn't very secure, to the point where he'd quit. Then she could look on her self-fulfilled prophecy and tell herself that Mike hadn't really wanted to change after all.

I could understand how Sharon felt. I appreciated the fact that she'd been frustrated for a long time. There was no doubt in my mind that Mike's insecurities, and the way he tried to cover them up with defensive aggressiveness, had caused her a lot of pain. In her place I would be resentful, too. Like her, I might not get too excited over my partner's first tentative efforts to change. I might be a little cynical, and inclined to slap the hand that reached out. I might be defensive, and reluctant to face up to the fact that I probably contributed to my own misery. I might also not want to face up to the fact that if I wanted things to get better, I would have to be an active part of the healing process.

People who hold grudges, who find it difficult or impossible to forgive, come from families that have those attitudes. Sharon thought this was true for her. She could remember times when past transgressions had been dragged up and thrown at her. It had happened a lot, and she always resented it. Despite how much she hated it when she had been the one on the receiving end, however, as an adult she modelled these very same habits. Once she realized that was what she was doing, it became possible for her to change. She didn't have to be just like her parents. She could choose to resist attitudes that were so deeply ingrained they seemed like second nature. This can be true for you, too.

For Sharon and Mike, the healing process got rolling once both of them understood that many of the attitudes that were hurting their marriage were attitudes they had modelled on their families. More than anything else, it was Mike's difficulties in being positive and open, and Sharon's tendency to hold on to resentments, that had led to the alienation between them. These attitudes weren't in their genes, but in their heads. Once they accepted that, they could take responsibility for both their attitudes and their behavior. They could see that they had a choice: to model self-defeating habits and attitudes blindly, or to resist them and find new ways to relate.

Changing is hard enough with encouragement; it's almost impossible without it. If you want things to be different in your relationship, if you want your partner to *act* differently, you're going to have to learn how to use encouragement to foster change. There's definitely a place for criticism in the change process. Sometimes criticism is the only way to make it clear what you don't like. But you need to follow criticism up with clear statements of what you *do* want, backed up by encouragement to support getting what you want.

The rules for encouraging change are simple enough, but using them on a day-to-day basis may not be so simple a task, especially if you're a person who comes from a family that relied more on criticism than encouragement, or on punishment more than reward. To encourage change means doing just the opposite: using praise more than criticism, and reward more than punishment.

Keep these rules in mind when trying to learn to encourage change:

Rule 1: Don't just let your partner know what you *don't* like, or what you *don't* want; let your partner know what you *do* like, and what you *do* want.

Rule 2: Use encouragement *more* than you use criticism to get what you want. Use every opportunity to praise your partner, and to express your appreciation for giving you what you want.

Rule 3: Use reward more than punishment. Do something to please your partner when your partner does something that pleases you.

Hidden Ambivalences:
What You Don't Know Can Hurt You

Ruth and Harry said they were in my office because they wanted to make one last effort to save a sex life that had been on ice for nearly a decade. That's how long it had been since they had made love.

Although they came in calling it a last-ditch effort, it was quickly apparent to me that neither Ruth nor Harry was in any hurry to get down to work. No sooner did I bring up the subject of sex than Harry remarked that he hoped I wouldn't take too narrow a view of things. What did that mean? I asked. Well, speaking for both of them, he replied, they hoped I wouldn't focus *only* on sex. Did that mean, I asked, that they weren't feeling ready to talk about sex? No, he quickly replied, blushing. They just didn't want to be pressured into doing anything before they were ready for it.

Listening to Harry, I got the feeling that if I pressed them, this couple might not show up a second time. In my mind I could picture them, commiserating with each other over how I'd "pushed" them. On the other hand, if I did nothing they might conclude that seeing me had been a waste of time. All in all, I felt, I probably couldn't win. So with minimal expectations, I went ahead.

My initial impression was that it was Ruth who was the most uptight about being there, and especially about being pushed into sex before she was ready for it. She sat in her chair with a stony expression on her face, and said little other than to indicate that she was flatly, intensely resistant to the notion of having physical contact of any kind with Harry. As they described their relationship, it became apparent that there was not only no sex, but no longer any physical component to their marriage at all. There was no hugging, no kissing, almost no touching of any kind as far as I could tell. Ruth openly admitted that she didn't like it when Harry tried to kiss her, or even touch her for that matter. Kissing, she said, turned her off, casually adding her opinion that men's bodies, generally speaking, were ugly. She no longer undressed in front of Harry, but preferred to do her changing in the bathroom, alone.

Ruth's attitudes revealed what you could call an *open ambivalence* about sex. She very definitely had mixed feelings, to say the least, about physical intimacy. But, equally important, she was up front and frank about it. That way I at least knew what I was dealing with.

Harry, on the other hand, was harder to read. He was so protective of Ruth that it made me uncomfortable. He took the position that he was eager to rebuild their sex life; but he was *so* understanding about her reluctance to being pressured into anything, *so* willing to wait. I couldn't help wondering if he was really so sincere. I decided to reserve judgment until I got to know him better.

As you might expect, Ruth's negative feelings about sex had not come out of the blue. There was a history behind it, and that history pretty well accounted for why she'd become turned off. Suffice it to say there had been a lot of frustrations. She summed it all up once when she said, "I began to feel that each time we made love, Harry had this list of things I was supposed to do to him. But there wasn't much effort on his part, to do anything for me. Naturally, I started feeling angry. But when I complained, he'd get all uptight, and then we wouldn't talk for days. So I figured it was better just to drop it. The only problem was, my sex drive dropped, too."

To my surprise, we got past those first moments, and therapy actually progressed, albeit slowly. Not wanting to push too hard, I spent much time filling in the details of Ruth and Harry's relationship. I started getting the clear sense, as time went by, that Ruth was loosening up. She was talking more freely, smiling more often, and had started mentioning sex. I pursued this, trying to get them to talk to each other about what had gone wrong.

Our first real breakthrough came when Ruth began confronting Harry with her pent-up frustrations and resentments. I encouraged this, telling them that confrontation, unpleasant as it was, could open the door to involvement and intimacy, and maybe even to sexual passion for Ruth.

Harry talked about how much he liked it when Ruth was open and honest. Even if it meant that they had more fights, he said, he wished she were more open about her feelings. I heard his words, but I felt uneasy.

It wasn't long after this phase of our work, when Ruth began to come out of her shell and started confronting Harry, that I discovered Harry's *hidden ambivalence*. What's that? Simply, it means that no matter what he said, Harry had some decidedly mixed feelings about the changes in Ruth, which he wasn't owning up to. He also had mixed feelings about resuming their sexual relationship, which he wasn't owning up to, either. He'd been keeping these feelings hidden behind Ruth's more up-front resistance. That's the essence of hidden ambivalences: they are expectations and motivations that lie behind the scenes. Often they're concealed behind someone else's more open and obvious ambivalences. They can spell real trouble, because if you either don't recognize them, or else try to avoid dealing with them, they can easily sabotage your relationship.

What were Harry's hidden ambivalences about? What were his secret feelings and expectations? For one thing, even though years had gone by and he was now supposedly older and wiser than he was when his sexual relationship with Ruth had started, he really wasn't any more sexually experienced than he had been back then. He wasn't any more secure about himself as a lover, either. In fact, he was a lot less secure. His secret fear was that he wouldn't be able to satisfy Ruth sexually.

Harry also had some secret expectations of his own. In his heart he really wanted Ruth to pursue him, rather than having to pursue her. He like being made love to, but the truth was that he had never felt all that comfortable about women's bodies, and he felt anxious making love. Secretly what he would have liked was for her to get over her sexual "block," to want to make love to him again, but to have few expectations of him.

If we hadn't uncovered Harry's hidden ambivalences and brought them out into the open where we could face them and deal with them, I had no doubt that his mixed feelings about what we were doing would sooner or later have undermined any progress we could have made.

Detecting Hidden Ambivalences

To get started on understanding and working through hidden ambivalences, you first need to figure out if they're there. To do that, you need to look out for these *signs* of hidden ambivalences.

Sign 1: Withdrawal and Denial
By far the most common signs of secret fears and hidden expectations are withdrawal and denial. When your partner clearly seems to be avoiding you, acting cold and distant, but denies that anything is bothering him or her, there's a good chance that hidden ambivalences are at work.

Sign 2: Passive Aggressiveness
"Passive" aggressiveness is aggressiveness that's hidden behind a veneer of innocence and good intentions. Its most common forms include making excuses for not doing something that was promised, "forgetting" commitments that were

made, and subtly putting someone down while denying any hostile intentions. The aim of passive aggressiveness is hostility: but the passively aggressive person won't admit it. You feel hurt, or angry, but they act innocently. The more you find this happening to you, the more likely it is you're bumping up against hidden ambivalences.

Problems of sexual desire and intimacy are rarely purely individual matters. More often than not, and particularly if the problem has developed over a period of years, when a couple falls out of love both partners are involved. In your relationship, which one of you has the more open ambivalences? Which one of you is the more likely to be harbouring ambivalent feelings or expectations that are hidden away?

Confronting Hidden Ambivalences

Once you are fairly sure that your partner has feelings he or she is holding back, or expectations he or she is not expressing openly, the next step is to try to uncover them. Hidden, they aren't doing anyone any good. They're breeding resentment in both of you. With hidden ambivalences, you don't know what it is that you're dealing with, what the other person really wants or feels. In relationships, what you don't know *can* hurt you. So you need to do whatever you can to get your partner to tell you what he or she wants (but won't say), or feels (but won't express). Here are some hints for doing this:

Rule 1: *Don't Pretend*
Don't pretend that hidden ambivalences aren't there. When you feel that your partner is obviously withdrawing, but denying that anything is wrong, don't go along with this cover story. If you do, you're only playing into the problem. Instead, keep the pressure on. Say things like: "I don't think you want to talk about it, but I definitely feel that something's bothering you, and you're not telling me." Don't let

your partner convince you that it's all in your head. Chances are your gut feelings are pretty accurate. If it *feels* like something is wrong, something probably is.

Rule 2: *Say "Ouch!"*

If withdrawal, or passive aggressiveness, is hurting you, *say so*. Don't suffer in silence. Even if your partner denies any intention of hurting you, let him or her know that you're hurting. And let them know what they did, or said, that hurt.

Rule 3: *Be Ready to Listen*

If you succeed in getting your partner to open up a little, try not to discourage that by reacting defensively to the first words they say. Try to hold back your own reaction until you *listen*. Discover what their hidden feelings or expectations are. Remember, hearing them out will put you way ahead of where you were when you didn't know what the problem was.

Rule 4: *Identify Feelings and Expectations*

Keep two questions in mind. You need answers to them to have an idea of what you're up against. First, you need to know what your partner is *feeling*. Most likely they're angry. You need to know: angry about what? What did you do, or not do, that got them frustrated or angry? That leads to the second issue, and question: What do they *want*? That gets you into expectations. You can't move on to the last step until you know what your partner's expectations are.

Rule 5: *Negotiate and Compromise*

By the time you've finished this book, the words *negotiate* and *compromise* should be etched in your memory. That's good, because they really are the keys to establishing an egalitarian relationship, which is the only kind of relationship that can sustain intimacy and sexual passion over a lifetime. If you won't negotiate over expectations, if you can't learn to give and take, then you may stay stuck where you are, forever.

PART III

Getting in Touch

In Part 3 we look at body image and sexual fantasy and how these things relate to sexual desire. Being able to sustain sexual interest in marriage, we've learned in earlier chapters, is dependent on being able to maintain intimacy and involvement, and on minimizing barriers such as resentment.

Sex and intimacy are not independent of each other. There can be many motives for making love, but one of them surely is intimacy. Sex is one way to experience intimacy. How much we want to pursue this form of intimacy depends a great deal on the quality of our relationship, but it also depends on how we feel about ourselves as physical and sexual beings. This is the subject of Part 3. You will learn here how your attitude about your body plays a key role in your ability to get close, and how to get in touch with your sexual desire. ❦

7

Sexual Fantasy

Sexual desire doesn't pop out of thin air. It begins as an emotional *reaction* to something. Something we either see, hear, smell, or think triggers a sexy feeling in us. Our ability to think is critical to sexual desire, since often the thing that strikes a spark of passion is a thought or an image—sexual desire, in other words, often begins in our own heads.

Getting in touch with sexual desire begins with getting in touch with our ability to respond to sexual stimuli in the world around us, as well as with the unique capacity we have, as human beings, to generate our own sexual stimuli in the form of thoughts and fantasies. The essential difference between people with high sexual desire and people with low sexual desire is that one group recognizes and uses this potential, while the other group either ignores it or resists it.

Once you find yourself noticing and responding to sexual cues in your environment, or to sexy thoughts in your head, then the sexual-fantasy techniques described here will give you a way to turn those sparks of desire into a flame of passion, and to keep that flame burning until the time is right for action.

Sexual Desire: Biology Or Psychology?

If you think about it for a moment it's pretty obvious that your health influences your behaviour. Anything from a passing cold to a chronic illness can and does influence the way you feel. In general, the state of your health affects your state of mind. It can bring you up, or it can lay you low, and it certainly can influence how you feel about sex, including your level of sexual desire.

We also know that our bodies produce specific chemicals, called hormones, that play a role in sexual functioning. Inadequate hormone levels, like nervous-system damage and circulatory problems, can be the causes of sexual dysfunctions such as impotence. There is some evidence, too, concerning the role that specific hormones, like testosterone, can play in sexual desire. It seems clear, for example, that you can increase a man's sexual interest, at least temporarily, by giving him testosterone.

Does all this new data on the role of physical factors mean that psychological and emotional factors are not important in sexual desire? Are sexual dysfunctions and low sexual desire really medical problems? I don't believe this information should be interpreted that way. What it means is that we shouldn't be naïve about the fact that our bodies *and* our minds can be the causes of sexual difficulties.

Sexual desire may be partly a matter of biology—but only partly. Sexual passion may have an instinctual quality to it, but it isn't just an instinct. Sexual desire, much more than sexual performance, is something that we as human beings have the unique ability to create. We can foster it or stifle it, flow with it or flee from it. We do one or the other depending on how we feel about ourselves, how we feel about being sexual, and how we feel about the person we're with.

In approaching problems of sexual desire, it's important to begin with the assumption that we are *all* sexual. Not only do I assume that all people are sexual, but I also assume that women and men are *equally* sexual. Both men and women have the ability to influence their own sexuality. They have the power of sexual choice. They can either accept or reject, enhance or stifle, their own sexual potential.

Having sexual desire is mainly a matter of facilitating and utilizing the sexual potentials that are already there inside you. Conversely, having low sexual desire typically means that you are blocking your own sexual feelings, that you are choosing not to utilize your capacities. Anxiety, anger, guilt, shame, or some other emotion incompatible with sexual passion is usually what's in the way. People with low sexual desire react to sexual cues or thoughts with one of these interfering emotions, instead of with sexual excitement. Why? There can be many reasons. They might, for example, feel disgusted about their own sexual urges, because they were taught that sex is dirty and immoral. Or they might be anxious and ashamed about sex because they were abused at some earlier age. Or they might be feeling alienated and angry with their partner, and not *want* to let themselves feel turned on by that person.

When this kind of pattern repeats itself often enough, it can develop into a strong and automatic habit. The long-term result is that a person loses touch with any sexual feelings that were there to begin with. Instead of realizing that they've cut off their sexual desire, though, they often conclude that disgust, anxiety, resentment, or guilt is the *only* feeling they have when it comes to sex. Instead of saying to themselves, "I could be turned on, if I wanted to be," the message they give themselves is "Sex is disgusting," "Sex is wrong," or "Sex is scary."

Sexual desire rarely comes over us so suddenly and strongly that we're swept away by it. Though there may be times when passion can overwhelm us, these are usually rare moments in our lives, leaving memories that stand out. Sexual desire usually begins at a much less intense level. Most of the time it's more of a spark than an explosion. And usually we create it ourselves.

The first sparks of sexual feelings can happen in response to all kinds of things. People differ greatly with respect to what turns them on. For some, it may be a certain kind of smile; for others it's the curve of a leg; and for others still, it may be the sound of someone's voice. I met a woman who told me that she was turned on by a man because of the way he laughed, another who responded only to thin men, and one who was crazy about beards. One man I knew thought his wife's breasts were just about the sexiest things he'd ever seen; another didn't care so much for breasts, but could get very turned on by long brown hair and dark brown eyes.

If we keep our senses open, there's practically no limit to the number of potentially erotic stimuli in our world. But that's the key phrase: *keeping your senses open*. People who are in touch with their sexual passion do just that. Their sexual responsiveness is open to the world.

People with low sexual desire avoid paying attention to things around them that could strike a spark of sexual desire. This may be a strong habit eventually, but initially it's a choice they make. Changing this pattern, so that a person becomes open instead of closed to sexual stimuli in their environment, can do wonders for a stalled sex life.

The other thing that people with low sexual desire *don't* do is generate their own sexual feelings using thoughts and fantasies. Not only do they put blinkers on themselves in terms of what they see, but they put blinkers on thier minds.

When I suggest to someone that they really do have a sex drive but that they've failed to develop or use it, they sometimes act offended. To them, it seems like there's nothing there to develop, nothing to use. They feel put down or misjudged. I understand that. I put them on the spot, and I know it. I make them responsible for their own sexuality. My intention isn't to make them uncomfortable, though, so much as it is to get them in touch with their innate capacity for being passionate. What I'm trying to tell them is that they really do have a lot more potential and ability than they think they do.

Resisting Sexuality

Humans are uniquely gifted in their ability to fantasize, but they don't always choose to use that gift. Through fantasy we have a way of freeing ourselves from the constraints of reality. As far as sex is concerned, fantasy enables us to control our own sexual arousal. Through fantasy we can strike a spark of sexual interest. Or we can take a weak sexual feeling and develop it into something stronger. Thanks to our imaginations, we can turn ourselves on, or take a passing sensation and build it into a driving urge. Alternatively, we can resist sexual feelings and turn ourselves off.

Men and women who complain of sexual disinterest may not indulge in much sexual fantasy. They may fail to make use of this vital tool for creating and enhancing sexual feelings. Andrea, for example, was someone who was so anxious and guilty about her sexuality, and who avoided it so well, that she ended up believing she had no sex drive at all. After working together for a while, we concluded that there were two main reasons for this. First, she'd been raised by parents for whom sexual strictness was probably a compensation for guilt over their own sexual behaviour, since we guesssed that Andrea's mother was probably pregnant when she got married. That much we established quickly. But there was a second factor at work, which came to light only much later.

From the time she was a young girl, Andrea's mother seemed intent on smothering her daughter's sexuality. Until she was nearly sixteen, Andrea was kept in bobbed hair and baggy pants. The few new clothes she had were usually bought in the boys' section of a local department store. She had one dress, and two skirts, which she wore only to church on Sundays.

Andrea was never allowed to wear make-up. She couldn't remember her mother ever saying that she looked pretty. There were never any positive conversations about boys or dating; on the other hand, there were frequent negative comments about men and what they were after with women.

As you might expect, Andrea grew into a young woman who

had a lot of confusion about sex, and a lot of anxieties about men. The only words of wisdom she'd ever heard at home on the subject was that men were all the same, always out for just one thing, and that good girls didn't give it to them. She got the distinct impression that "good" women didn't really enjoy sex, but submitted to it only to fulfill their marital obligations.

On the day before she was due to leave home for college, Andrea got a lecture from her mother that she never forgot. She remembered her father, standing there in the background, nodding in agreement as her mother warned her to watch out for the boys at college. "Especially those fraternity boys," her mother said, "with all their lies and their filthy minds." With these words playing in her mind, Andrea packed her bags and set off on her own for the very first time in her life.

No sooner did she get to campus than Andrea realized she was more than a little out of step with her peers. The most obvious difference was in their wardrobes. They wore clothes that were a lot tighter, a lot more colorful, and a lot more sensual than anything she owned. Then there was their language: it was coarse to her ears. They talked frankly and without embarrassment about men's bodies, about sex. They even laughed about it. Andrea felt uncomfortable with their behavior, but she found herself liking the women a lot in spite of it.

It wasn't long before Andrea began experimenting with different ways of dressing and talking. She tried wearing make-up, and went to her first parties. In this new environment, her sexual feelings got stirred up. Up until then she had been more or less sexually dormant. She had never masturbated, never had so much as a single sexual fantasy, or even a sexy dream that she could recall. Now and then, starting when she was about twelve, she had experienced periods of agitation. She called these "the fidgets." Whenever she had a case of the fidgets, she found that the best thing was a long hot bath.

By the start of her second semester Andrea's curiosity about men was beginning to overpower the anxieties that her mother's words had instilled in her. Until then she went to parties with friends, dancing and having fun, but steering clear of one-to-one interactions with men. Then one night she abruptly shifted gears. Acting on an impulse, and under the influence of more wine than she should have had, she decided to let her friends go back to the dorm without her, while she went off with someone she just met. He seemed friendly enough.

Her friends didn't realize just how naïve Andrea was. They let her go. She ended up in a strange apartment, sitting in a living room waiting for this guy to return from the other room with the cup of coffee he had promised her. He came back instead carrying nothing and wearing an open robe.

Andrea's rape was not physically violent, but emotionally it was devastating. You can imagine the effect it had on her budding sexuality. Afterward she was filled with guilt and shame. Like many victims, she told no one what had happened to her that night. For years afterward, though, she was plagued by periodic nightmares, and suffered anxiety attacks that woke her in the middle of the night, her sheets soaked with sweat. Sometimes she'd cry out in her sleep.

After the rape Andrea stopped going out. To explain the sudden change in behavior she made up a story about a boyfriend back home. She got into the habit of changing dormitories every semester. By the time she graduated, four years later, she had not had another date. She also had not made a single close friend.

About a year after she was out of college and working, Andrea changed gears again, abruptly slipping into exactly the opposite pattern. She started going to singles' bars, where she drank a lot and picked up men. Usually she would go to bed with them that same night, and never see them again. Sexually she was tense and slow to arouse, if she got aroused at all. Usually she went ahead with intercourse even though it was painful, then faked an orgasm.

About a year later, Andrea got married to the first man who asked her. Then, after a year of making love to him every night, she suddenly announced one day that she didn't want to have sex any more. She didn't even want to be touched any more. Ever. Full stop.

At first John tried being patient. But he wasn't a patient man, and his tolerance quickly ran out. Then he got mad. When Andrea didn't respond to coaxing, he got tougher and demanded sex. This worked for a while. It got him sex—not very good sex, but then sex with Andrea had never been great. When even that stopped, John's last desperate stand was to threaten divorce. He would leave, he said, unless Andrea got over whatever sexual hang-up was plaguing her, and soon.

It was a different story, but with the same ending, for Peggy. She, too, was turned off to sex, though not so much out of shame as anger. We're already familiar with the wall of pent-up resentments that can come between a couple. In Peggy's case, sexual desire had become locked up behind that kind of wall of anger. Like Andrea, she didn't believe she had a sex drive at all. She never thought, fantasized, or dreamed about sex. She never felt "horny," never wanted to be touched. She claimed that she hadn't always been that way, though, and she blamed her husband Don for what had happened to her.

In some sense Peggy was right: Don was partly to blame for her loss of sexual interest. Early in their relationship, she was sexually eager and affectionate. But she was frustrated with their lovemaking. Don suffered from premature ejaculation, but he wasn't willing to do anything about it. Whenever Peggy said she was unsatisfied, or hinted that she wished he could last longer, Don would get angry. Things would get better, he said, if Peggy could just relax more. He flatly rejected her suggestion that they get some help. So Peggy decided to give it some time.

In many ways Don and Peggy's marriage was a good one. As compared to some men she knew, Peggy felt that Don was considerate and kind, and she thought twice about stirring up trouble by complaining too much about sex. But time went by, and sexually things didn't get better. She started finding it more difficult to ignore her frustrations, more difficult simply to wait and hope that Don would change. Her resentment started to reveal itself. She found herself becoming critical, started picking on Don in lots of ways. Naturally, he was offended. As things got worse he started saying that she was a castrating woman. There was an incident that ended up with him walking out for two days. That scared Peg, and she tried to tone down her criticisms; but inside she didn't feel any different.

The end result of all this was mutual alienation. After a while there wasn't much overt fighting going on, but there was a coolness and distance in their marriage that I could feel from the first time I sat down with Don and Peggy. By then it wasn't just one person who'd built a wall of anger. At that point both of them had good cause to feel angry. It was true enough that Don had been defensive and unreceptive to Peggy's suggestions that they go for therapy. Maybe he'd even started it all by being so defensive about sex. But it was also true that Peggy had become cold, critical, and rejecting. Each of them felt justified in their resentment, but that wasn't going to get either of them anywhere.

Part of the dynamics of both Peggy and Andrea's loss of sexual desire was the fact that they eventually came to the point of actively resisting their own sexual feelings. They weren't born this way, but had developed resistance over time. In Andrea's case the resistance was the result of shame and anxiety; in Peggy's case it was anger and resentment that had led to avoidance. In one case the roots of the problem lay in the past; in the other case the causes could be traced to the present relationship. The common denominator, however, was the *resistance* these two women had developed to anything that might strike a sexual spark in them. They never looked at men, and they never indulged in sexual fantasy. In short, they stopped themselves from responding sexually to their environment, and they didn't use their innate abilities to get turned on. They eventually concluded that they had no sex drives. What do you think?

Sexual Fantasy: Right or Wrong?

Some people are prejudiced against sexual fantasy. They reject the notion that sexual fantasies are a normal part of a person's sexuality, a natural way that people have of turning themselves on. Instead, they take the attitude that fantasizing is somehow abnormal, just as some people believe that masturbation is abnormal. For them, there are "right" ways and "wrong" ways to inspire sexual desire, and fantasizing happens to be one of the wrong ones.

A person like this might say something like, "It's wrong to be married to one person but to have to think about someone else in order to get turned on." Or, they may believe, and fear, that sexual fantasies are invitations to trouble: "Thinking about someone else might make me want to *do* something with someone else."

What about the idea that it's morally wrong to fantasize about someone besides your partner? There are people who take the attitude that it's okay to fantasize so long as your fantasies are about your own partner and not about anyone else. They might also say that it isn't right to be having sexual fantasies while you are actually making love to your partner—that you owe your partner your undivided attention when you're in bed together. It seems wrong to them to have your attention on anyone but your partner, or on anything but what's right in front of you.

I get concerned sometimes if someone tells me that they make love but *never* think about the person they're making love with. I wonder what it means for a relationship when one partner finds that the only way they can have sex is if they're thinking about somebody besides the one they're in bed with. I can get a little uncomfortable, too, when someone says that they *always* need to fantasize in order to get sexually aroused or to reach orgasm. But these are unusual cases, and I really haven't run into them often. My thought about them is that in these cases one partner may be using fantasy to avoid the other. Fleeing into fantasy may be a sign that there are some unresolved issues in a marriage. But other than for these extreme cases, I see nothing wrong with using sexual fantasy as *one* way to get turned on, or to stay turned on. Human beings are naturally gifted with imaginations, and it seems pretty silly to decide *if* we should use them, or *how* we ought to use them.

Sometimes people can feel uncomfortable not so much about having sexual fantasies but about the *kinds* of sexual fantasies that turn them on. Usually, what lies at the heart of these anxieties is a secret suspicion that sexual fantasies are signs of sexual perversion. People often believe that they are highly unusual for enjoying the kinds of fantasies they do. Secretly they suspect that they're perverted, or at least neurotic, and some spend a great deal of time and energy trying to figure out how they developed their "weird" sexual preferences.

One man I worked with was particularly disturbed about his sexual-fantasy life. What bothered him was the fact that ever since he was an adolescent he'd masturbated to fantasies in which he played the role of a woman making love to several men. He was more or less disgusted with himself over the fact that no matter how many times he tried, he couldn't break himself of the habit of using this fantasy when he masturbated and occasionally when he was making love to his girlfriend. When I asked him if he thought his fantasy meant anything, he said he was sure it meant he was a "latent homosexual." He felt this way even though he had never had sex with another man, and had never wanted to.

I could understand why Harry was upset about his sexual fantasies. After all, we live in a macho and homophobic culture. Imagining that you're a woman making love to a group of men just isn't the kind of fantasy that most men would be proud to own up to.

In talking things over, Harry and I began to get some ideas about where his sexual fantasies might have had their origins. Most likely they had their roots, we decided, in the fact that this well-developed, handsome, and athletic man had actually been sickly, thin, and weak as an adolescent. In school he liked to hang around with the "jocks," even though this group didn't accept him easily. These "jocks," Harry knew, attracted girls a lot more than he did. That made Harry feel pretty inadequate, but it also attracted him to them.

It was around this same time, in high school, that Harry first started masturbating to fantasies that he was a pretty girl seducing "jocks" and having sex with them. I suggested to Harry that he may have chosen to identify with the female rather than the male role in his sexual fantasies, simply because of his own feelings of inadequacy. Since he didn't believe he could measure up to the ideal of the "jock" image, in his fantasies he put himself in the role of a woman instead.

I suggested to Harry that his sexual fantasies might have no secret "meaning" at all, then or now. They didn't necessarily say anything about his sexual orientation—didn't necessarily mean that somewhere deep down he was gay. They could simply reflect his envy of the "macho" image he felt unable to fulfill. Rather than fighting them, I suggested that Harry let himself use his imagination and enjoy whatever fantasies turned him on. That worked very well. He soon reported that sex with his girlfriend was better than ever, and that he no longer gave much thought to what he was focusing on when he made love, but simply enjoyed himself.

Answering the following few questions can help put you in touch with any resistances you may have to using your sexual imagination.

- Do you feel that it's wrong to enjoy sexual fantasies?
- Do you have sexual fantasies that make you feel uncomfortable or ashamed?
- What do you fear that your sexual fantasies might mean about you?
- Would you be willing to try taking the attitude that your imagination isn't something you can control completely, that you might be better off using it than fighting it?

Fears of Losing Control

Does sexual fantasy represent temptations that can lead us into trouble? That's an interesting question. Put another way, the concern that some people have is this: Can indulging in sexual *thoughts* cause you to lose control of your sexual *behavior*? A lot of people who have negative feelings about fantasy seem to believe this. Underlying their anxieties about sexual fantasies are fears of losing control of their sexual behavior. Fearing that they could be overwhelmed by them, they ward off all sexual thoughts. They act as if they believed that sexual passion is an irresistible force that can be set free by sexual fantasies, and which has the ability to overcome your own will, overrule your judgment, and sweep you away.

Although I'll grant that sexual desire can sometimes come on strong, our sexual behavior is never beyond our control. We always have a choice either to pursue or not to pursue a sexual interest. People who argue that they can't control their sexuality, like people who say they can't control their anger, may be looking to justify their actions without taking responsibility for them, or excuse behavior that's gotten them into trouble.

People who are afraid to let themselves think sexy thoughts, for fear that they'll lose control and act on them, are usually sitting on some unresolved issues in themselves or their relationships. It's like the parent who feels so angry at a child that they're afraid to touch them, for fear of losing all control of their anger. That kind of anger takes time to build up. Usually it's been brewing for some time. The latest incident, the one that pushes them over the edge and makes them scared of their own anger, is only the last straw, the proverbial crack in the dam.

So it is with fears of sexual fantasies. If someone has been sexually frustrated in a relationship for a long time, so that sexual tensions have built up to an intense level, they might have reason to fear that they couldn't keep the lid on any longer if they let themselves indulge in some sexually stimulating fantasy. They fear that they might vent their frustrations at their partner, or look to satisfy their sexual needs outside the relationship.

People who fear their own sexual fantasies are afraid to let themselves feel sexual. They need to realize that it isn't so much their sexual fantasies that are causing their trouble, as the situation their relationship may be in. What they need isn't to avoid sexy thoughts or feelings, but to confront their fear of their own emotions, and whatever issues they're avoiding.

People who resist their own natural emotions, like sexual passion, not only get out of touch with the feelings they avoid, but usually also develop a fear of those emotions. If you avoid getting angry, for example, you'll probably also develop a fear of your own anger. Why? Partly, because of your *inexperience* with it. If you don't have enough experience with anger—with feeling it and directing it appropriately—you won't feel confident in your ability to handle it. You just don't know where it will lead you, or whether you'll be able to manage it. By avoiding it, anger becomes foreign territory to you, emotionally speaking, and you shy away from it. The same goes for sex. If you're inexperienced and insecure about it, you may be inclined to avoid it.

An even more common reason why people develop fears of their own emotions, particularly anger and sexual desire, is that they don't want to face up to issues that those feelings are likely to bring up. They don't want to face up to what they're angry about, or why they're sexually frustrated. On some level they usually know why they're angry or frustrated, but they don't want to risk confronting it. So they try their best to steer clear of thoughts and situations that can evoke those feelings.

What kinds of issues do people avoid by "losing" their interest in sex? At times it may be a conflict within themselves that they are running away from—conflicts, for example, over their sexual orientation. More often, though, it's problems within a *relationship* that lie behind low sexual desire.

Gentle Ben

Ben had "lost" his sexual desire many years before he came to see me. He was a big, handsome, bearded man. When he sat, he made the chair he sat in look small. His style of talking was slow, deliberate, and thoughtful, so slow in fact that until I got used to them I found the long silences in our conversations unsettling. He made me think of someone who had just stepped out of a log cabin in the deep woods.

What impressed me about Ben was his willingness to shoulder all of the blame for all of the problems in his sixteen-year marriage to Karen. "I don't know for the life of me," he said, "what that woman sees in me." He described himself as a reclusive person who had no close friends and didn't like people. "I don't have a single close friend. I don't think I've ever initiated a single social engagement in my life, and certainly none since we've been married. Karen does all of that. I just go along. And then I'd just as soon go home early."

Ben also saw himself as an inadequate and uninvolved father. "Karen says that she's had to raise our three boys all by herself, and I've got no right to criticize her. I have to admit she's basically right. All I do—all I've ever done—is work. I make plenty of money, but you know how it is—no matter how much you have, it never seems to be enough. There's always something more to be done, something else to be paid for. If it isn't toys, it's bikes. Those boys love me, but sometimes I wonder why. I'm never around"

"Tell me about your sex life, Ben," I said.

"Well," he replied, "there isn't much to tell. I never had much experience in that area. Karen says I don't understand what a woman needs, and I suppose she's right. I want to satisfy her, but I can't seem to do it. Except for in the very beginning, I've never been that interested in sex. I suppose that's been frustrating to her, too."

As we discovered over the course of several months, Ben's tendency to shoulder blame so easily was his way of avoiding conflicts in his marriage. Similarly, not thinking about or wanting sex was his way of avoiding having to confront his own sexual frustrations. He'd rather take the blame for everything, I learned, from tight finances to his sons' problems in school, to his unhappy sex life, than confront anyone, especially Karen, about them. He could honestly say to me that he never got angry, and never felt sexual passion. I felt certain that was because those kinds of feelings could lead to conflicts.

For Ben, getting in touch with feelings, both sexual feelings and angry feelings, meant having to face possible conflicts with his wife: conflicts about the kids, about money, about sex.

Is being out of touch with your feelings a cover-up for possible conflicts you might be avoiding? Ask yourself the following questions:

- Do you have concerns about what becoming more sexual might lead to?
- Are you afraid of your own sexual feelings?
- What sorts of things about your partner's behaviour and attitudes in general would you like to change?
- What sorts of things about your partner's *sexual* behaviour and attitudes in particular would you like to see change?
- Are you afraid to confront problems in your relationship in general, or in your sex life in particular?

Whatever it is you're avoiding, avoiding it is not going to make your relationship, or your sex life, any better. It's not going to make you feel better about yourself, either. On the contrary, the longer you avoid, the more hopeless your situation will seem, the more depressed you will get, and the more you will hate yourself. Why not take a chance and start communicating instead of holding back? Why not come forward, instead of withdrawing? It worked for Ben, and it could work for you.

Exploring Sexual Fantasy

Over a period of years, several techniques have evolved from my work that people have found helpful in learning to use their natural gift for fantasy as a tool to explore and develop their sexual interest. These techniques aim to teach you to create your own sparks of sexual desire, to be able to take a weak sexual feeling and build it into something stronger, or to keep a sexual flame burning until the time is right.

The Sexual-Fantasy Journal

One approach that some people have found helpful is to begin a sexual-fantasy journal. A sexual "fantasy," incidentally, does not have to be anything elaborate. Something as small as a passing sexual thought or daydream qualifies as a sexual fantasy. Of course, it can be fun to experiment with taking one of those passing thoughts or daydreams and developing it into something more elaborate.

A sexual-fantasy journal can be grand or modest, depending on your personal taste. Some people enjoy making it into something special. They might buy an attractive diary book and use it just for this purpose. Others use any old pad or scrap of paper that's available. I've read sexual fantasies that were written in diaries with leather bindings and silk bookmarks, and others that were written on lunch bags.

Whatever you choose to write your fantasies on or in, make sure that you feel they will be safe and private. Remember, this is your personal journal; it's not for public distribution. A few people who did this exercise felt better about it only after they bought themselves diaries with locks on them. Most people, though, feel okay if they simply have a safe place to keep their journal. Obviously, it's important to feel reassured that your privacy will be respected by your partner. Talk about this ahead of time if you have any doubts or concerns, and come to an agreement.

The rule for keeping a sexual-fantasy journal is simple. *Use it as a place to jot down all the sexual thoughts, daydreams, night dreams, and other kinds of sexual fantasies you have.*

Make your journal entries on a daily basis, preferably at a time when you don't feel rushed. Try not to cut corners—write down *all* of the sexual thoughts, no matter how brief, that you can recall having that day. Be sure to date your entries, so that you can keep track of your progress in developing your fantasizing ability. Here are some hypothetical examples of entries that could appear in one day:

Monday, September 3

- Found myself noticing Sheila's legs this morning as she walked through the office. She has nice legs. That made me think of June, who's got nice legs, too. Started feeling a little turned on.
- Heard a dirty joke this afternon, which made me think about Sheila and June again. Found myself thinking about having sex with June or Sheila in one of those swinging-singles hotels.
- Was watching television and saw that actress I like. Felt really turned on and wished I was with someone I could make love to right then and there.
- Had a dream last night that I was having sex with somebody I didn't recognize. She had a beautiful face and nice legs, and we were having a great time even though we didn't know each other. We seemed to have some trouble, though, finding places where we wouldn't be disturbed.

When they first begin keeping their journals, people usually expect them to be empty. Then they're surprised at how fast they fill up pages. Typically they find that the longer they keep their journals, the longer their entries get. The first day or two there may be only one or two short notes. If they persist at it, though, by the end of two weeks there is plenty of material in their journals.

Try keeping your sexual-fantasy journal daily for two to three weeks. After that period of time, take an hour or so some evening to look it over. Notice how many entries there are, and whether there are more now than there were when you began. Were there any days that went by without you having at least *one* sexy thought? Did you find yourself starting to feel turned on now and then while you were fantasizing?

The two most important things that a sexual-fantasy journal can do for you is to show you that you really do have a capacity to create sexual feelings, as well as to respond with sexual feelings to things you see and hear. This is all there is to a "sex drive."

Once you've worked on this level of sexual fantasy for a while you may be ready to move on to something bigger and better.

Expanding Sexual Fantasies

A variation of the sexual-fantasy journal involves taking some of your fantasies and elaborating on them, in your head or on paper. Start by going through your journal and choosing two or three fantasies that you really enjoy. Now, take one of those fantasies that involves a sexual scene and expand on it. Take that one scene and build it into a full-length motion picture in your head. Imagine the scene, and then imagine what came before it. Where did the lovers meet? What led up to their romantic and sexual involvement with each other? How do they feel about each other, sexually and otherwise? Elaborate on their lovemaking, adding anything you like that would make it more pleasurable.

Sexual fantasy is your private tool for getting and staying sexually turned on. Your imagination is a natural gift that you were born with. Learning to use that gift can do great things for you; ignore it, and you ignore your own sexuality. You don't have to share your sexual fantasies with anyone, unless you want to. Respect the privacy of your partner's imagination, as much as you'd want him or her to respect yours.

❦   ❦   ❦

Another variation of sexual fantasy is something I call the *erotic masterpiece*. To do this exercise you will need a pad of paper and at least one solid hour without interruptions. Find a place and make yourself comfortable.

Spend this hour (or more) writing out your fantasy of an exciting sexual encounter. Make sure that what you create represents *your* idea of what's erotic. Be as graphic or as vague, as pornographic or as romantic, as you want to be. Put yourself in your story, or make it a story about someone else. Whatever you do, don't create something that you think someone else would find exciting, unless you also find it exciting. If in doubt, ask yourself this question: Is this exciting to *me?* If it isn't, rewrite it to your own taste.

There are two problems that people are likely to encounter when trying to write erotically, and the first has to do with writing for yourself versus writing for others. People get themselves into trouble when they try to force their own sexual responses into some kind of mould - in other words, when they try to get turned on to something that might turn somebody else on, but not them. They get caught up in the idea that something *ought to* turn them on, when in fact it doesn't. Meanwhile, they may ignore things that really do stir their sexual interest. When you're doing this exercise, therefore, try writing for yourself, not for anyone else.

The second problem that people often have is overcoming their own shyness about writing something erotic. They may enjoy reading books or stories that turn them on, but they feel embarrassed about creating their own material. For this reason, getting started on your erotic masterpiece may be difficult. It might take some persistence to get past your initial shyness. Once you do get over this hurdle, you may be surprised at how well you can get in touch with what turns you on, and how you can put it down on paper.

Priming the Pump

Something I call *priming the pump* is the last technique we'll talk about that can be used to help you begin to develop your sexual imagination. It's simple enough to do. Just read a selection of erotic fiction written by others, in books or in magazines. The goal is to help you get started with your own fantasizing. Countless writers have tried their hand at this kind of writing, and it isn't difficult to find.

Visit the library, or your local bookstore, and browse until you find one or two books that seem to have some sexy passages in them that turn you on. Again, make sure that what you read appeals to *you:* don't waste your time on something that you think would appeal to most people, unless it also appeals to you. Some people, for example, like steamy, explicit erotica: others are turned on to something more romantic, less explicit.

Spend some time reading the erotic literature that turns you on. It shouldn't be long before you're able to start creating your own sexual fantasies, and using them to strike your own sparks of sexual desire.

Appearances Can Be Liberating

What does the word *sexy* make you think of? What kind of a gut reaction do you have to that word?

People whose sexual desire is blocked can have more or less negative attitudes about the idea of being sexy. They may feel embarrassed about it, anxious or guilty about it, or disgusted by it. When I asked one woman to tell me what she thought of "sexy women," she responded with words like "cheap," "promiscuous," and "dirty." From men with low sexual desire the most typical reaction I get is discomfort or embarrassment over the idea of being sexy.

Negative attitudes about being sexual are revealed not just

by what people say, but in the way they look, and especially in the clothes they wear and the way they groom. We all have ideas about what makes us look good, and people with positive attitudes about their sexuality enjoy looking attractive. But we also have some boundaries that we can't cross without feeling uncomfortable. People with low sexual desire have very rigid boundaries in this area. They can go so far to avoid looking *too* sexy that they actually camouflage their sexuality. This has the effect of making others react to them differently—as nonsexual beings. It also helps them to smother their own sexual thoughts and feelings.

I was seeing a couple once with another therapist, and in the middle of one of our sessions my co-therapist, Leslie, casually brought up the issue of the way the husband, Ken, dressed and groomed. This couple was seeing us because of *his* lack of interest in sex.

Once Leslie pointed it out, I was really struck by just how much Ken "dressed down." He wore old-fashioned shirts, and baggy slacks which were full of creases. He was about as out of style as you can be. His shoes were old and scuffed. His hair looked as if it was cut without so much as a passing thought to how it looked and, to make matters worse, it was plastered down using one of those old-fashioned greasy hair tonics. He wore no jewellery, and his belt and tie looked as though they were a thousand years old. He didn't dress this way purposely, only thoughtlessly. He really had no sense of the way clothes made him look (or feel), much less the way others would react (or not react) to him on a sexual level.

While Leslie talked with Ken about his clothes and the way he groomed, I began thinking about myself. I half listened to their conversation while mentally reviewing the contents of my closet. I decided that I could stand to buy a couple of new pairs of slacks, and maybe some shirts. I stole glimpses of myself in the room's one-way mirror, and decided that I should also invest a little more next time I needed to get my hair cut.

Leslie suggested that Ken think about having his hair cut and styled. I nodded in support and approval. She said he should think about getting himself a couple of new shirts, some new slacks, some ties, and some shoes. Again I nodded. She suggested that he take his wife along when he went shopping, and let her help him choose clothes that were more stylish. I thought about that.

"Maybe you could even pick up one or two things that are a little sexy," Leslie said. Ken blushed, and while I was thinking about whether I owned any sexy clothes, Leslie succeeded in pushing him into making a commitment to do it.

When Ken arrived for our session the next week I almost didn't recognize him. Instead of the usual faded old button-down shirt, he was wearing something new and neat looking, which fitted his lean body for a change, instead of ballooning out around it. For a moment I thought he had gone out and bought a hairpiece, but it turned out he had only stopped using the greasy kid stuff. He was wearing new shoes, and a smart belt complemented his tailored slacks. Last, but not least, I noticed that he was wearing his shirt open at the collar, instead of buttoned to the neck as was usual.

What was even more amazing than this transformation in Ken's appearance was the fact that he reported that *changing the way he dressed had changed the way he felt.* What Leslie had done, he said, was to give him permission to do something he had always secretly yearned to do. He always knew that he was uptight about sexuality, and that he even dressed in an inhibited way. But it wasn't until Leslie brought it up that he felt he could let himself do something about it.

A few weeks after this breakthrough session, Ken approached his wife sexually for the first time in years.

Does it seem hard to believe that something so simple and obvious as the way we dress or the way we comb our hair can affect our sex drives? It may seem like a trick, like something too good to be true but if you think about it, it makes sense. Perhaps more important than that, it works. If you doubt me, try it for yourself. Follow these simple steps:

Step 1: Think of three or four ways in which you could change the way you dress, or the way you groom, that would be *sexier* than the way you dress and groom right now.

Step 2: Try making *one* of these changes each week, for three or four consecutive weeks. See if this doesn't have some effect. I think you'll find, as many others have, that looking sexier can make you feel sexier.

I'm not suggesting that the cure to problems of sexual desire is sexy clothes, or a new hairstyle. But I am suggesting, though, that this little exercise often works, almost like magic.

8

Body Images

Sexual Pride

America's obsessive preoccupation with thinness has led us into an epidemic of eating disorders. On college campuses the situation is so severe that at times whole dormitories get caught up in crash diets, bizarre eating fads, or the use of laxatives or vomiting as means of controlling weight. The syndrome of alternate binging and vomiting, called bulimia, can develop to a point where it threatens its victim's health.

In one way or another, the diet craze has affected all of us. We are all more or less self-conscious and insecure about our appearance. Feeding our insecurities is the modern visual media, which bombard us with images of thin bodies that are billed as ideals of sexual desirability.

A healthy body image, or what I call *sexual pride*, is essential to intimacy and a healthy and lasting sex drive. In contrast, a poor body image stands as a barrier to intimacy and sexual passion. When a person feels shame or embarrassment, instead of pride about his or her body, they will stand back and shy away, instead of coming forward and getting involved. A poor body image puts us one-down, when what we need is to feel equal.

Sexual pride facilitates both intimacy and sexuality. Feeling good about your body is a critical condition for feeling good about being sexual. Rejecting your physical self, on the other hand, leads to rejecting your sexuality. That's why you so often see a correlation between a deteriorating physical condition and a deteriorating sex drive. As body images deteriorate, so often do relationships. People with poor body images pull away from others and become unsexual and alienated. They avoid thinking of themselves as sexual, and they avoid sexual feelings. Eventually, they may avoid wanting to get close or involved at all.

Assessing Your Body Image

Sometimes a poor body image can be the result of excessive modesty. Some people actually think more of themselves than they're willing to admit publicly. If that's you, fine. More often, a person's negative comments about the way they look mean just what they suggest: self-rejection. If that's you, then you need to confront your attitude toward yourself, and either change it or change yourself. You absolutely have to do this if you hope to keep sexual passion alive.

While there are always things we can do to make ourselves feel better about our bodies, often the problem lies more in our failure to identify and appreciate the physical assets we do have.

Before going on, take a few minutes to answer the following questions for yourself:

- Name the three most attractive things about you, physically speaking.
- What have you gotten compliments about most often?
- Do you think you have a sexually attractive body?
- Which aspects of your physical self evoke the most negative reactions in you?

- Are the negatives—the liabilities you see in yourself—balanced by your physical assets?
- Are there one or two parts of you that you dislike so much that you might be blind to your personal assets?
- If you had done this exercise five years ago, would your answers have been different? If so, why?

To explore the relationship between body image and sexuality, try answering these questions:

- Can you believe that someone else might actually be attracted or turned on by a part of you that you don't like? Can you accept this attraction as genuine and normal?
- When you look at yourself in the mirror, can you imagine someone being sexually attracted to what you see? If so, what are your most attractive personal (physical) assets today? What physical assets could you improve?
- If you imagine that it would be difficult for someone to be attracted to you physically, why do you feel this way? What in particular do you think others would be turned off by? Is it possible to change this?

Sexuality, Illness, and Disability

Major illnesses can have lasting effects on sexuality. The same is true for surgery and disability. Sexual taboos once stood in the way of open talk between health professionals and their patients on matters of sexuality. Doctors felt uncomfortable asking their patients about their sex lives. At the same time, they hesitated to ask questions they felt unqualified to answer. To them—and to many doctors today—questions about intimate relationships seemed beyond the scope of medical practice.

But the state of our health and the quality of our relationships *are* related. The family doctor may not have all the answers, but if the doctor is interested, that at least gives patients the message that their concerns about the impact that illness or surgery has on their relationships, and on their sexuality, are legitimate ones. And that's a message many patients need to hear.

I can understand why doctors and other health professionals feel uncomfortable talking to patients about sex and the consequences of illness, surgery and disability on their patients' sex lives. It can be a very uncomfortable conversation. I remember one experience in particular that brought this home to me.

My interests in the impact of illness on sexuality had led a colleague and me to develop a research project on that subject. Toni and I were interested in interviewing men and women with serious medical conditions, like kidney disease, and people who had undergone certain types of surgery, such as hysterectomies, in an effort to understand the ways in which their illness or surgery had affected their feelings about themselves, their lifestyles, and their sexual relationships.

We were still in the early phases of the project when the phone rang early one afternoon. It was Toni. She told me that a nurse in the Obstetrics and Gynaecology unit of a local hospital had called her, asking if someone could come over and talk to a woman who wanted to see a counsellor. She asked me if I wanted to do it together. "Yes!" I responded eagerly. "I'll be right over."

I remember the room. It was large, bland, and quiet. Uncomfortably quiet. The only noise was a slight buzz that came from a small black box that sat atop a tall stainless-steel pole beside the one occupied bed. The air was heavy with an antiseptic smell. There was the usual hospital-room furniture—vinyl and wood— surrounded by barren walls painted a glossy off-white color. Bouquets of flowers had been placed randomly around the room, some on tables, some on windowsills, others on the floor. The door closed behind us with a soft whoosh. I began to feel my stomach tighten. The thought ran through my head that maybe I shouldn't have been so eager to do this.

The bed had been cranked up so that the woman in it lay in a semi-reclining position. She was connected to a number of tubes. In addition to the machine on the stand, there were two monitors sitting on a table beside her. They had small red and green lights that glowed. I wondered what happened when something went wrong. Did the lights flash, did an alarm go off? I hoped I wouldn't find out.

We'd been told her name ahead of time: Marsha. I also knew that only a few days before she had undergone emergency surgery for removal of a massive pelvic tumor. The tumor was huge and had been growing fast, so fast that as little as an hour or two could have meant the difference between life and death. The surgeons had saved Marsha's life, but her body wasn't the same.

Toni said hello, her voice echoing in the room. I sat down in one of the vinyl chairs. I sat quietly, suddenly very grateful that Toni was there.

Toni asked Marsha how she was feeling, and if she was very uncomfortable. Then she asked Marsha about the surgery, starting with how it came to be that she needed emergency surgery.

Marsha told her story to Toni, who listened attentively. Once or twice Marsha glanced over at me. I did my best to seem calm and tried to smile reassuringly, but I knew I was feeling nervous and that it probably showed.

Marsha explained how she had gone to her doctor, who examined her briefly and immediately called an ambulance. She was rushed to the hospital, where several vials of blood were drawn and an intravenous line was inserted into her arm. She was in a lot of pain, and she was feeling scared. She knew that her condition was serious and that maybe she was even going to die.

After all the tests were rushed through and finished, a doctor had come into Marsha's room and told her the conclusion. He said that surgery was needed. He described it all—how big the tumor was, how fast it was growing, and what would have to be done. He made it clear that it was an emergency. Then he asked her to sign a release, giving permission for the surgery. Her husband, who'd been out of town on business, still hadn't arrived. The doctor said there was no time to wait for her to talk to him. Marsha signed.

"What were you thinking when he explained all of that to you?" asked Toni. "It must have been pretty scary."

Marsha looked at Toni. She smiled weakly. "Yeah," she replied, "I was scared, all right. But you know what I was really thinking about while he was describing that surgery to me?"

"What?" asked Toni.

"I was lying there thinking, this is the end of my marriage."

Toni and I glanced at each other. "Why did you think that?" Toni asked.

"Well," said Marsha, "I thought, after this my husband will never be able to have sex with me again. Probably he won't even want to touch me. I've made love for the last time in my life— that's what I thought. And that maybe we'll even end up divorced."

I was shocked. I couldn't believe, back then, that a person facing death would be thinking about sex, much less about divorce. I've learned a lot since then. It's not so unusual at all. Heart attack victims, women who face mastectomies, people on renal dialysis, and others, all wonder and worry about their sexuality, and their relationships. They fear the loss of their sexual attractiveness, and they anticipate the worst for their marriages.

As bleak as things sounded at that moment, I'm happy to say that life really wasn't over for Marsha. A couple of months after she left the hospital, she called Toni and made an appointment to talk some more. This led into regular counselling, first for her, and a little later for her and her husband. Once he got involved, and once Marsha got over her own emotional reactions to the surgery, things started to work out for them. It wasn't all smooth going, but it wasn't as downhill as Marsha had expected, either. To rebuild a sex life following such a great trauma, she need a loving and committed partner. Fortunately, she had one. Equally important, Marsha had the courage to confront her own shame and embarrassment and to rebuild her sexual pride in spite of physical trauma. This wasn't easy, but it was possible.

❦   ❦   ❦

A good body image is a starting point for a healthy sex life. Sexual pride, in and of itself, will not guarantee you a successful sexual relationship. It won't guarantee that sexual desire will last, or that your relationship will be an intimate or happy one. On the other hand, *without* a healthy body image, the chances of these things happening are almost nil. Sexual pride, in other words, is part of the foundation of healthy sexuality. Like intimacy, it's a *condition* for healthy sexuality, and it needs attention.

You might say that the case of Marsha was unusual—that individuals like her have exceptional reasons to have a poor body image. That's true. Still, experience has taught me that the amount of anxiety Marsha felt may be different from your own only by degrees. And the effects of a poor body image, whether it's the result of surgery, genetics, or simply lack of exercise and nutrition, are surprisingly similar: it undermines sexuality and intimacy.

Body Images and Abuse

Before we move on to the subject of building sexual pride, we need to talk about one more important cause of body-image problems, and that's abuse. Abusive relationships can be as traumatic to a person's body image as the most severe illness, surgery, or disability. Abuse can be outright and obvious, as in sexual assault or molestation; alternatively, it can take on forms that may be more subtle but no less harmful.

Betty was one of those girls who have to deal with the problems caused by an early puberty. Like most girls in her situation, she quickly became self-conscious about her breasts and figure. From age eleven on she had had to endure stares and lewd comments, not to mention bad jokes. She felt uncomfortable just walking past men, especially groups of them. To try to minimize the problem, she learned to camouflage herself. She wore bulky sweaters, bulky coats. But even that didn't always work.

As if this kind of abuse wasn't enough, Betty's body-image problems were compounded by her coarse and lecherous father. He was one of those men who seem determined to frighten their daughters away from all other males. He took delight in embarrassing people with his brazen sex talk. The more inappropriate the occasion—like over the dinner table, or in front of guests—the better he seemed to like it. He'd laugh when everyone else blushed and fidgeted in response to his jokes and language. He justified his crudeness in the name of sex education. "I just want my kids to know which way is up," he'd say. "I don't want them getting themselves into trouble."

Part of Betty's "sex education" consisted of having to listen to her father go into great detail about the ways that men tried to take advantage of women. "I know you don't want to hear this," he'd say time and time again. "But you just mark my words. One day you'll see. Some fella will come on to you, all sweetness and light. But as soon as you let your guard down—and you will—then you'll be in for the surprise of your life! Then you'll see what life is all about, what men are really after."

Betty's father never physically molested her, but he did abuse her by his talk, and also by the way he looked at her. One incident in particular stood out in her mind. It happened on a Saturday. She was about twelve, already developed, and already self-conscious about her body. She'd just taken a shower and was headed toward her bedroom wrapped in a long towel when her father stepped out of his bedroom and into the hallway.

As usual, she didn't like the way he was looking at her. He stood there, staring at her as she walked by, in that way that made her skin crawl. She avoided his eyes and tried to slip quickly past him and into her room. She did, but he followed her, closing the door behind him. She turned, clasping the towel to herself.

For a brief moment Betty had an urge to call out, to scream, but then she got control of herself. Why didn't she scream? For the same reasons that most victims of childhood abuse never call for help: they're either too embarrassed or too afraid to.

Her father stood there, across the room, for what seemed like an eternity, looking at her. His eyes wandered up and down the length of her body. She remembered how fast her heart was beating, and how she felt frozen, unable to move or talk.

Betty had felt uneasy around her father for a long time, but this was the worst thing that had happened yet. She wanted to cry. She wanted to run. Most of all, she wanted her father to go away, and she didn't know what she would do if he didn't.

He sat down on the edge of her bed. She looked at the door, gauging the distance. He saw her and laughed, as though he knew what she was thinking. Again, she avoided his eyes, though she felt them on her. Finally, he spoke. "You know, Betty," he said, speaking slowly and deliberately, "sometimes you make your dad feel like a dirty old man." Then he got up and left.

Betty's father never laid a hand on her; so, was she a victim of abuse? She was. She may not have been physically beaten, or physically molested, but she was abused. Her father's talk and lewd behaviour had the effect of taking an already self-conscious young girl and making her feel scared of men and ashamed of her body. Instead of having opportunity to get used to her body and its changes, and to like it, she was made to feel nothing but anxiety and embarrassment about it. There were many times she wished she could literally walk away from herself. It was no surprise that she developed into a woman who feared men, who had bad feelings about her body, and who believed that she could live happily without sexual relationships at all.

Building Sexual Pride

A healthy body image begins in childhood. It starts with a healthy body, but it depends a great deal also on how we're treated. Affection, praise, respect, and an acceptance of sexuality are needed if a healthy body is to evolve into a healthy body image. In contrast, victims of sexual abuse, and people who are raised in environments that lack respect and acceptance, usually feel ashamed of their bodies.

At some time in our lives most of us have probably lacked one or more ingredients of a good body image. Some of us, for instance, have suffered illnesses or accidents that have threatened or injured our sexual pride. The psychological consequences of illness or surgery can easily outlast the physical ones. Similarly, people who went through fat periods earlier in life, or who were sickly for a time, can suffer from self-doubts long after fat or illness are gone. The adult who is fit and trim may be concealing a poor body image that had its roots in an adolescent fat period or a sickly childhood.

An awful lot of people can benefit from some boosting of their body images. We're living in a youth-oriented, appearance-oriented society. We love the visual media, and with each succeeding generation that media dominates our lives and shapes our attitudes more and more. It's a media that's naturally given to appearances, and to presenting the superficial aspects of life better than it can present what lies beneath the surface. It emphasizes seeing more than listening. It often sacrifices depth for novelty. It keeps our attention not by engaging our interest in one subject for any length of time, but by moving from subject to subject every few minutes.

The visual media presents basically one model of physical attractiveness, and it bombards us with that image over and over again. There is a certain male body type that's presented as attractive, and a certain female body type. Everyone then goes around trying their best to make themselves look like that. In one way or another, we all fall short. The result? Anxiety, self-doubt, and insecurity—in short, body-image problems that find their way into our sexual relationships and cause trouble.

In reality, people aren't nearly as limited or uniform in what they find sexually attractive as the media images suggest. What people really find attractive in another person may be very different from the media ideal. I remember one couple for whom this was poignantly true. It was a marriage between two people who were about as different from the media ideals as you can get. He was skinny, short, and wiry. She was tall and fat. If you compared these two to the media ideals of what's sexually attractive, you'd have to conclude that there was no way they could possibly be turned on to each other. But they were. The only problem was that both of them had body-image problems that got in the way of letting themselves be as sexual as they felt, or of accepting the other person's sexual interest. This is usually true of people with body-image problems: *they are insecure about their own sexuality, and they question the sexual interest of others.* Both of these people fit that bill. They felt inadequate and unattractive, and they couldn't bring themselves to believe that the other person's interest in them was genuine. They held back a lot, and they both had "low sex drives." Of course, the truth was that they both had plenty of drive, but lacked the confidence to pursue it.

What makes a person "sexy" and attractive goes deeper than appearances. We're turned on to a person not only because of the way they look, but the way they act and other qualities they have. Even so-called "flaws," in other words, variations from the media ideals, are frequently turn-ons for lots of people. This becomes apparent when you talk to someone about what *really* turns them on, and when they answer you honestly. Under these circumstances people have talked to me about the way they're turned on by their wife's hairy arms, or by their husband's big nose. I've also listened to people talk about the kinds of personal qualities in another person that arouse them sexually, qualities like kindness or aggressiveness, extraversion or playfulness.

Good Body Images

The essence of a good body image is a belief that you possess *physical* qualities that others can find sexually exciting. What may seem like inadequacies or flaws to you may be genuinely appealing to someone else. That appeal is not a sign of some sexual perversion on that person's part, but simply a reflection of the fact that beauty truly lies in the eyes of the beholder. If you can believe that about yourself, you've got the beginnings of sexual pride.

To begin building a better body image, you can try to identify the factors that may be contributing now, or that may have contributed in the past, to a poor one. Here are some of the most common causes of body-image problems. How many of them describe experiences *you've* had?

- Lack of physical affection in your family.
- Too little praise and too few compliments about how you looked when you were a child and adolescent.
- Physical illness, surgery, or disability you've suffered at some point in your life.
- Sexual abuse or physical abuse.
- Rape or attempted rape.
- Rejection of sexuality in your family.

To build sexual pride *now*, it's essential that you get these things behind you and start taking a fresh look at yourself. This begins with healing old wounds.

Healing Wounds

After you've identified some things that may have hurt your body image and stood in the way of your ability to develop sexual pride, the next step is simple: *find someone you can talk to about it.* Emotional wounds are healed when we open up and share painful feelings with someone who cares about us and likes us. If you want to let go of the past and build a new future, it's essential that you find someone to share your pain with, so that you can bury it.

One of the keys to the healing process in sharing has to do

with the fact that we are strengthened by someone who doesn't reject us, even when we reject ourselves, and who understands and accepts the pain and anger that we feel. This acceptance enables us to let go of the past. Without it, you can stay trapped in the past forever.

Some people look to therapists for help with healing emotional wounds. If the therapist is accepting, and if he or she truly cares, then therapy can be effective in healing and rebuilding. But a therapist isn't necessary. In fact, if the therapist is *not* accepting and caring, therapy can make matters worse instead of better.

I can't count the number of times that I've told a client something he/she has heard before, from a friend, a lover, or someone in their family. For some reason, when I say it they believe it; but when it comes from someone else, they don't believe it. Coming from a spouse, a sibling, or an old friend, they write off positive comments to blind love, or assume that they're being benevolently lied to. Have you done that?

So long as you don't discredit the support that friends, lovers, and family have to give, these people can be every bit as helpful as a therapist. Despite what you might think, these people may be more honest with you than you realize. If you reject them, and their caring, you could be standing in your own way.

Think about sharing your self-doubts and insecurities with someone close to you, someone whose opinion you value and who you think cares about you. Take a chance on letting them know about whatever guilt, shame, or anxiety you feel. If you're the victim of past abuse, try sharing your experience with someone you love and trust. See if it isn't true that the caring of others has the power to heal old wounds.

Your Photo Biography

As an aid in the process of opening up, you might want to make up something I call a *photo biography*. To create it, you'll need some old family photos, plus some more recent pictures of yourself. If you can't find any pictures of yourself, you can probably count that as more evidence of your body-image problem.

Your collection of photos is the raw material for your photo biography. You'll need to edit this collection, selecting only a few pictures from several different ages, starting with childhood and working your way toward the present. Lay out your biography on a tabletop according to the following scheme:

FRIENDS	ALONE	FAMILY
	(Younger)	
	—	
	—	
	—	
	—	
	—	
	(Older)	

Your goal is to create a picture history of yourself, beginning when you were younger and working your way up to the present. Your photo biography should capture you at different ages, and in different settings. Include formal as well as candid photos that marked occasions like birthdays, school photographs, and family picnics. Try to include photos of yourself from each of the following time periods: preschool; early school years; middle school years; early and later secondary school years; post school years; mid-twenties; late twenties; early thirties; mid-thirties; late thirties; etc.

At each age, try to choose one or two photos that show you alone, and others that show you with family and friends.

Your photo biography can be helpful as something you simply go over by yourself, looking at yourself at different ages and linking what you see to how you felt about yourself at the time. In this way you can trace changes in your body image over the years.

It can be even more productive to share your photo biography with someone else. Go through each picture, and try to recall your life at that time. Describe your family, your classmates in school, and your friends. Tell a friend what you think you were like, and how you felt about yourself.

Can you remember changes, as you go through your biography, in the way you felt about yourself at different times? Were there ups and downs? What was associated with those times when you felt *worst* about your body and your appearance?

Go through your biography again, but this time identify those times when you felt the *best* about your body. What was the source of that pride—was it your appearance, some ability you had? If you didn't feel good about yourself then, what can you find in these pictures to feel good about *now*?

As you look at yourself in this perspective, are you aware of a progression in your appearance, from the childlike to the adult? Did you feel more, or less, like an adult at that time when you were *physically* making the transition from childhood to adulthood?

What were your thoughts and feelings about sex at different points in time? When did you begin masturbating? When did you have your first sexual fantasy? When did you have your first sexual experience with someone else? What was this like for you? Did you feel attractive to this person?

When were you the happiest with your own body? *Imagine, just for a moment, feeling really good about yourself—feeling that there are things about you that someone else could find attractive and appealing, in the way you look and in your personality.* Hold on to that feeling for just a moment before you let it slip away.

Getting in Shape

The fact is that a healthy body gives you more cause to feel proud than an unhealthy one. Illness and disability can make it harder to build and maintain a positive body image, but they don't by any means make it impossible. The key is to make the most out of your physical assets, whatever they are. An "able" body is no assurance of a good body image, if that body is neglected.

Taking care of your body boils down to two things: exercise and nutrition. I am neither a nutritionist nor an expert on physical conditioning. But I don't believe you have to be either in order to develop basically good eating and exercising habits. What you do need is an appreciation of what poor nutrition and lack of exercise can do to you. Together these things affect every aspect of your life, from your stamina and energy level, to your resistance to illness, to your general sense of well-being. They can definitely have effects on intimacy and on your sex life. That's right, your *sex life*. It takes energy to make love, and a neglected body usually doesn't have that energy.

We know from people who are experts in nutrition and exercise that proper exercise and diet can help everyone, from those who are already basically healthy, to those who have suffered major illnesses such as diabetes or heart disease. One researcher, for example, studied the effects of exercise on men who have had heart attacks. He placed one group of these men on a daily exercise program, using a bicycle-type machine to develop their physical fitness gradually. Their exercise was tailored to their condition. Nobody was asked to push too hard too soon.

A second group of men, who have also had heart attacks, were not placed on the exercise program. After sixteen weeks, the two groups were compared, not only for the effects on their hearts at rest, but for the effects on their hearts *while they were having sex*. The results? The men who had been on the exercise program were able to have sex with less heart strain. Their heart rates were lower, and their bodies were more efficient users of oxygen. In effect, sex was less physically demanding on them.

These results are dramatic and encouraging. Imagine what might be accomplished if proper exercise had been combined with good eating habits and a proper diet! And if a mere sixteen weeks made such a difference for men after a heart attack, what could regular exercise do for you after a year?

Before you go out and spend a fortune on exercise equipment, or start a crash diet, you owe it to yourself to start out with an honest assessment of your current state of health. Consult with your physician, get a thorough physical if you haven't had one for a long time, and get some professional advice about what you should and shouldn't do. Nutritionists and physicians with an interest in exercise are your best sources of advice. Don't expect great advice (or encouragement) if your doctor smokes and looks terribly out of shape!

Based on sound advice, you can set some realistic goals and formulate a reasonable plan of action. You want to determine not just where you want to get to, but *how fast* you want to get there. Don't be in too much of a rush.

Remember: *sensible dieting and exercise don't mean making yourself into someone you're not.* A healthy body isn't necessarily an ultrathin body, any more than it's an ultramuscular body. Don't set your own goals on the basis of fashion magazines, diet soda ads, or muscle-man movies. Try keeping in mind that getting in shape means looking *your* best, not looking like someone else. Body types differ a lot, and the media ideal of physical beauty is limited to one particular body type that might or might not be yours.

Looking Good

A fallacy that many people live by is the idea that you need to feel good about yourself *before* you will put much effort into *looking* good. Their reasoning goes something like this: If a person looks bad, it must be because they feel bad about themselves. Before they can start looking good, therefore, they need to start feeling better about themselves.

I go along with this thinking only about halfway. It's true that a person who looks bad probably doesn't feel good. Someone who neglects their physical condition and their appearance won't feel good about themselves or their sexuality. At the same time, it isn't true that feeling good necessarily has to come *before* looking good. On the contrary, *making yourself look better can make you feel better*.

You can test out my theory for yourself, first by following the advice in the last section on getting in shape. Next, you can start doing something about the way you look. That includes the clothes you wear and the way you groom. Follow the guidelines on clothes and grooming, and see if you start feeling better about yourself within a month.

Guideline 1: Clothes

Take stock of the contents of your closet and begin the work of feeling better by *getting rid* of all the old things you never wear, as well as those things you do wear that don't look good on you. Take the time to try things on and look at yourself in the mirror. Take your collection of frumpy clothes and *donate* it to a worthy charity.

Go out and buy yourself some new clothes for *work*, and some new clothes for *play*. Regardless of the kind of work you do, you should have two distinct sets of clothing: one that's appropriate for work, and another that's appropriate for going out in your free time.

Hint: If you don't think you're very good at picking out clothes you look good in, take a friend shopping with you—a friend who you think has good taste in clothes.

Guideline 2: Grooming

Aside from the clothes you wear, the other essential thing you absolutely must pay attention to is the way you groom yourself. In particular, you need to pay attention to your *complexion*, your *hair*, and your *teeth*. First, make sure that your hair is cut and styled regularly by a professional. You don't need to spend a fortune on this; on the other hand, don't just go to the barber or hairdresser who charges the lowest prices. And whatever you do, *don't* have friends, spouses, or relatives style your hair. If balding is hurting your sexual pride, look into getting a hairpiece, or better still a hair transplant. Don't skimp on either. Make sure you take your time and that you like the results.

It's surprising how many people neglect one of their most important physical assets: their skin. If they want to, a person today can spend a fortune on cosmetics that claim to stop aging. Even the names of some of these concoctions are funny, not to mention their claims. It isn't necessary to go to this extreme to take basic good care of your complexion. Just be sure to wash yourself every day, in a bath or shower, and use a good soap. If you like, a little cologne can be a nice finishing touch—but don't overdo it.

Last, and far from least, are your teeth. It's amazing how people can neglect their teeth, yet wonder why others are turned off by them. Decay, bad breath, and discoloring of your teeth not only affect the way others react to you, but you can bet they affect the way you feel about yourself. Basic dental care, like basic hair and skin care, should not cost a fortune, and doesn't need to become an obsession.

Thirty-Day Guarantee

If you follow all of the above guidelines, and make a good start in each of these areas, you will start to feel better about yourself in *thirty days or less*. Included in this change of attitude will be a change in your attitude about yourself as a sexual person. Guaranteed.

PART IV

The Heart of Love

What does it take to be able to stay in love? What's the key to intimacy and sexual desire? Is there some magic ingredient, some chemistry that a lucky few have, while others don't?

There may not be any secret ingredients or magic potions, but there are things that definitely do play a role in our ability to get close and stay close to another person. Staying in love requires commitment, but it goes beyond commitment. The essential elements of romantic love—intimacy and sexual desire—thrive and last in relationships where partners treat each other, and where they feel, like equals. They seldom last long in relationships that are lopsided: where one partner is one-up, and the other is one-down.

Obviously, not everyone has the kind of relationship that leads to lasting intimacy and passion. Understanding how important it is to have that kind of relationship, and what you can do to move your own relationship in that direction, is what you need to know.

Lasting love is built on a foundation which has two cornerstones, and they are *self-esteem* and *trust*. People who have problems of self-esteem, or who have difficulty trusting, will invariably also have difficulty placing themselves on an equal footing with someone else. In the first case, they won't feel confident enough to become an equal; in the second, they won't risk the vulnerability of equality. Sooner or later their relationships suffer from problems of intimacy, sexual desire, or both; in other words, they fall out of love.

Learning to understand low self-esteem and distrust, and how to eliminate them as barriers to intimacy and sexual desire, is the subject of Part IV. ❦

9

Self-Esteem

If self-esteem seems to you like something that relates to individuals more than to relationships, think again. The reality is that the quality of your relationship has a great deal to do with your level of self-esteem, and that of your partner. If even one of you suffers from low self-esteem, it's likely that your relationship will suffer from problems of intimacy, and sooner or later from problems of sexual desire, too.

Problems of self-esteem may be relatively easy to overlook in the early stages of a relationship, but they become more and more difficult to overlook as time goes by. Staying in love, much more than falling in love, depends on building and maintaining healthy self-images.

Self-Esteem, Intimacy, and Sexual Desire

What is intimacy? It's that "openness of interchange," that "spontaneous rebound of sympathy" that was quoted from Edward Carpenter's 1896 book back in Chapter 3. It's a deep mutual respect and appreciation. As one man put it, "I just want someone I can be myself with. Someone I don't have to put on a front with." That's a less poetic but no less accurate definition of intimacy.

Intimate relationships are open and spontaneous. That's partly what makes them special. Let's face it: in most of our day-to-day interactions with people, and even in many of our closer relationships, we're less than totally open. Intimacy is risky. We don't express everything we feel or allow ourselves to be totally spontaneous. That would leave most of us feeling too vulnerable. That's why relationships where we can be open are so special to us.

One thing that enables us to find the courage to be intimate is *self-esteem*, the subject of this chapter. People who have problems of self-esteem usually have a lot of trouble being intimate, too. Conversely, as they build self-esteem, their ability to be intimate is enhanced.

Intimacy has profound effects on us. It exerts its influence in literally every area of our lives, ranging from our sexual desire to our physical health. People who can be intimate cannot only be happier, but healthier. Relationships that are intimate nurture sexual desire, and people who can be intimate can live longer and better lives.

Does that seem like a wild claim? If so, consider for a moment the hard evidence. Consider, for example, the health statistics for people who are single or widowed, as compared to those who are in relationships. These differences are striking, especially for people over fifty. People who are alone are more sickly, and they die sooner. The data is overwhelming, and the conclusion unavoidable: loneliness is deadly.

Steve and Jenny came to see me for help with Steve's lack of sexual desire. The first thing that struck me as we talked were the differences, at least in the outward personalities, between these two people. Steve by and large seemed shy, quiet, and easygoing. Jenny, on the other hand, was obviously a ball of fire. She wasn't the least bit shy, and she had a habit of speaking her mind bluntly. She seemed to feel free to break in on the conversation whenever she wanted. She'd correct Steve in mid-sentence, and challenge him immediately on anything he said that she didn't agree with.

Aside from complaining that Steve wasn't coming on to her the way he once did, Jenny also complained that he had become withdrawn and depressed over the past year.

"How does Steve's depression reveal itself, Jenny?" I asked.

"Mostly," she replied, "it shows up in the lack of affection and sex. But also, the fact is that Steve has stopped talking to me."

"What do you mean? You mean he really doesn't speak to you?"

"He talks," she explained, "but not about anything important. Our communication has gradually dwindled to the point of chit-chat. I feel like he's purposefully avoiding talking to me about anything substantial. I really have no idea any more what's really on his mind or what's going on in his life, even when I ask him directly."

I learned that Jenny was particularly upset because Steve wouldn't talk to her about work. "You know," she said, "Steve is in a family business. Actually *we're* in it, is the way I feel. I've got just as much of a stake in it as he does. But he doesn't see that, or maybe he just doesn't want to see it. I'm as dependent on the business as he is. *My* future hangs on it as much as his. But I seem to be the only one in the family who's always left out. Everybody but me seems to know what's going on. If I want to know anything, I've got to call my sister-in-law. Do you know how embarrassing that is?"

As we got to talking more, I found out that Steve's loss of sexual desire, his withdrawal of affection, and his not talking about things all had started around the same time, and that was when some particularly difficult problems had cropped up at work. He was, indeed, a partner in the family business, but as it turned out he was the "least equal" partner. His father and older brothers exerted a lot more influence than he did.

About a year and a half earlier, the business had fallen on hard times, mainly due to competition from larger firms. To make matters worse, Steve had felt left out, from the beginning, of the decisions that were being made about what to do about the problem. It was at times like this that he resented his father and brothers the most. They acted as though they could run things better without him, could make better decisions without his opinion. He thought they underestimated him, but he never confronted them about it.

Jenny knew how Steve felt about work, and about the way his father and brothers overlooked and underestimated him. When the trouble at work first began, she understandably felt threatened. Her response was to want to know more than ever about what was going on, and to have some say-so, at least through Steve, about what was going to happen. But she was frustrated by the way Steve wasn't being included, and doubly frustrated because he refused to do anything about it. She vented a lot of her frustration at him. She pressured him to speak up, to assert himself and demand an equal say. Every night when he got home, she wanted to know what he found out, and whether or not he had confronted his father and brothers. Steve avoided that confrontation, and after a while he started avoiding Jenny, too. The more she pressed him, the more he backed off. The noisier her anger got, the quieter he became. As time went on he became less affectionate, too, and less sexual.

Holding back inevitably leads to depression and alienation, and that's exactly what happened to Steve. Not only did he feel resentful toward his father and brothers, but after a while also toward Jenny.

Steve suffered from low self-esteem. He lacked the self-confidence to confront issues and negotiate successfully for what he wanted. At work, what he wanted was an equal say-so in the business. But rather than deal with the issue, he avoided it. This made him feel resentful and, eventually, alienated from his family. It also made him feel bad about himself, which was why he was depressed.

At home Steve found no relief. Jenny's anxieties and demands to know what was happening, plus her continual pressure on him to confront his family, only made him feel worse. He wanted to tell Jenny to leave it, to get off his back. But he was afraid to confront her, too. His low self-esteem played a role in his marriage as much as it did at work. He'd always avoided conflicts with Jenny, and gave in rather than asserting himself and trying to negotiate a compromise.

As business got worse instead of better, Steve found himself having to work harder, but with no more input into the way things were being handled. His depression worsened. Jenny could tell that he was distressed, but by that point if she tried to approach him at all she found herself shut out. This led to arguments, more distance, less affection and intimacy, and less and less sex.

Jenny put up with this for as long as she could, but when her sex life went down the tubes she drew the line. She pressured Steve again, this time to see a therapist. That's where I came into the picture.

The problems between Steve and Jenny were obviously related to what was going on at work. But the depression he was burdened with, and the resentments he carried around with him, were the result of the fact that his basic approach to life was to rely more on holding back and avoiding than on confrontation and negotiation as ways of dealing with problems. He always felt one-down in relationships, whether they were with his father, his brothers, or his wife. As a result he also felt alienated from them.

The word *avoidance* sums up the typical coping style of the person with low self-esteem, and Steve was no exception. His self-doubts were far from crippling. In fact, he was really a very competent and talented man. But his low self-esteem kept him from getting more of what he wanted, and from having more of an impact in his relationships.

Why did Steve have low self-esteem? How had he learned to avoid instead of confront problems? Once I knew something about his family and background, those questions weren't hard to answer. It had a lot to do with his being the youngest, of growing up in the shadow of a egotistical and overbearing father, and having two older brothers who were nothing if not chips off the old block. Between them, Steve's father and brothers had ruled the roost. They got their way, and Steve, like his mother and sister, learned from an early age that arguing with those three was a losing proposition. From his perspective, confrontation got you nowhere. Trying to negotiate accomplished nothing. Privately, Steve confided in me that Jenny sometimes reminded him of his brothers and his father, and that as he got older that bothered him more and more.

The outcome of therapy for Steve and Jenny was a happy one, thanks to both of them. Steve really did possess a great deal of talent, brains, and energy. He could see these qualities in his wife, but not in himself. He had a perspective on the family business that was more objective than that of his father and brothers. He also had a lot of common sense, which they didn't. Once he realized this and saw how his role in the business had evolved into a mirror image of his role in the family, he became determined to do something about it. Seeing things from this new perspective, he couldn't be satisfied any longer to sit on his feelings and avoid conflicts at any cost.

Steve's first really assertive move was to decide to work in therapy alone, rather than with Jenny. He said he wasn't opposed to her getting involved later on, but for the time being he preferred to come in by himself. To her credit, Jenny saw the wisdom in Steve's decision and backed off. And with that decision, Steve started to build his self-esteem.

Within a month Steve had pretty much turned his situation at work around. Within three months things were on a different track at home, too. What enabled him to do this? Determination. Basically, what Steve did was to take the insight he'd gained from therapy—this perspective on his work and his marriage, and how similar his behaviour as an adult was to what it had been as a child—and made a decision to not stay bogged down in the past. He began making decisions, and letting his thoughts and feelings be known. He started confronting issues instead of avoiding them, and negotiating rather than giving in. Was this difficult? You bet it was! But it worked.

Let me give you a couple of examples of things that Steve did that helped build his self-esteem. At work, he called a meeting of the partners. It was the first time *he* had ever called a meeting, and it got their attention. At the meeting he told them that though the company had problems, its biggest problem was that it was being run like a family instead of like a business. He gave them his opinion that if they didn't start running the business like a business, it wasn't going to last through the generations the way they all hoped it would.

The outcome of that meeting was an agreement to hold weekly business meetings, which would include *all* the partners, and to begin making efforts at relating to each other, at work, as business partners rather than as family.

Steve also made some changes at home. First, he told Jenny that she was right, that as his wife she did have a vested interest in the business. He understood that she would want to know what was going on. She was a bright and perceptive individual. He agreed he ought to talk to her about it, and he made a promise that he would. On the other hand, he also told Jenny that he didn't like being grilled about work, or pressured into decisions. And he didn't like being interrupted while he was talking, he added.

The changes that Steve made gradually made him feel less one-down, and more equal, both at work and at home. As this happened he felt better about himself. His depression lifted, and he started feeling less intimidated by Jenny and more interested in getting close to her. He talked to her a lot more. Occasionally they had conflicts. But they also started having sex again.

The Roots of Self-Esteem

Self-esteem is something we either develop, or don't develop, as we grow up. It isn't something we're born with; rather, it's something we *learn*. What is it, exactly? It's an attitude we have about ourselves. Call it pride, or self-love. Basically it's a belief that we're fundamentally worthwhile and lovable. It's a belief in our competence, and in our being as deserving of happiness and a good life as the next person. It's the basis for feeling *equal* to other people.

Imagine a person with high self-esteem. What would that person be like? First of all, that person would believe that they are *lovable*. They would also believe that they deserve *respect*, and that their feelings and desires ought to count as much as anyone else's. Above all, they would believe in their right to pursue happiness and personal fulfillment. In their heart that kind of person believes in their own *power*, and in their right to make choices and set their own course in life.

As important as understanding what self-esteem is, is to understand what it *isn't*. Self-esteem is not the same thing as achievement. Making that distinction is important, because a lot of people (especially men) try to substitute achievement for self-esteem. They try to build a sense of pride, a feeling of being worthwhile or lovable, on a foundation of tangibles like money, degrees, or status. These are signs of success, but they aren't necessarily signs of self-esteem.

Self-esteem is more fundamental than achievement or success. It can make success possible, but the two shouldn't be confused. I remember one woman who tried to convince me that she would believe she was intelligent if she could get a Ph.D. I told her it struck me that there was something wrong with that reasoning. From my perspective, having self-esteem would mean that she would believe she was intelligent *whether or not* she had a doctorate.

People with self-esteem are not insensitive or immune to hurt or disappointment. They can feel just as bad as anyone else. In their hearts, though, they still believe that they're lovable, even if they get disappointed in love. They can believe in their own chances for happiness, even if they're not very happy at the moment. They have faith in their abilities, even when they may fail.

Where does self-esteem come from? It has its roots, of course, in our families. High or low self-esteem is something that gets passed down from generation to generation. You can think of it as part of your *psychological* inheritance, much the way the color of your eyes, or your physical build, are parts of your *biological* inheritance.

Children's levels of self-esteem are largely a product of their parents' attitudes toward them. The parent who treats a child with love and respect raises a child who feels lovable and self-respecting. On the other hand, a child who is treated as second rate develops a second-rate self-image.

Children model their parents. I was really struck by this in one man I saw. He was, beyond a doubt, one of the brightest, most creative and sensitive individuals I've ever met. He was also a classic example of how low self-esteem becomes its own self-fulfilling prophecy.

In his high school and early college years Mitch had shown promise as an actor; yet he gave up acting. He quit college before he had a chance to see where his talent might lead him. His life after that had been a story of restless wandering and aimlessness. On some level, though, his untapped potential must have haunted him, for when I asked him why he had come to see me, he replied, "I suppose I've finally come to the conclusion it's time to stop running and face myself, to face life. I can't keep going on this way. I'm beginning to feel disgusted with myself. I just turned thirty, and I realized that I'm in the same place I was ten years ago. I've been all over the country, and gotten nowhere. I need to learn to like myself, and I need to find a direction in life."

Mitch had all the classic signs of low self-esteem. He felt that he had little to offer and was basically not even a likable, much less a lovable person. He was inclined to avoid conflicts, thinking that he was probably either wrong to begin with, or that even if he was right he would end up losing. He had no faith in himself, which was why he gave up easily and lived day to day without any sense of the future. As soon as success became a possibility, his fear of failure went wild within him, and he would run away. He never had a successful relationship. His history revealed a tendency to run away as soon as the going got good.

For many years Mitch had rationalized away his aimlessness by thinking of himself as a rebel. This was romantic, but it wasn't true. Fortunately, even he wasn't buying his own line any more. "If I don't do something for myself, now," he said, "I know I'm going to end up without a relationship and without a career, and be forty years old. I think I'd hate myself if I let that happen without trying to do something about it."

Some of Mitch's low self-esteem was the result of his parents' attitudes toward him, and partly it was something he'd modeled. His attitude toward himself seemed very close to the attitude his mother, who'd raised him alone, had had toward herself. What happens a lot is that people who don't have pride can't seem to teach pride. As obvious as this statement may seem, it's worth emphasizing, because as parents we're often blind to the way our children's attitudes toward themselves mirror our own attitudes toward ourselves. We frequently don't realize how we hand down attitudes, like low self-esteem, from generation to generation.

In Mitch's case the dominant attitude in his family had always been one of defeat and insecurity. A heavy, depressing atmosphere pervaded his home. "It was like growing up under a cloud," he said, " or *in* it—a cloud that had singled out our family." There was scarcely a word of encouragement, not just for Mitch, but for *anyone* in his family. None of them, it seemed, was able to believe in themselves, or in each other.

Parents are the family leaders. In any group, when our leaders act discouraged, we lose confidence. When our leaders seem defeated, we feel hopeless. That was true for Mitch. His family was one of those that breeds chronic depression and hopelessness, passing it down from parent to child to grandchild.

Though Mitch's problem of self-esteem was more severe than Steve's, the two solved their problem in much the same way. In the latter part of this chapter, we'll look at some of the specific how-tos of building self-esteem.

Building Self-Esteem

The Case of Nasty Nancy

My work with one woman led to an interesting little technique that not only her but many others since then have found helpful. It's simple enough, yet it can be very powerful if you're trying to bring yourself up from a place of low self-esteem. The key is to take the time to use it *consistently*. To introduce it, let me begin by telling you the story of "Nasty Nancy."

Nancy and her husband Jim were referred to me by a colleague for a last-ditch effort at marital therapy. Jim had recently asked Nancy for a divorce. I got the impression that he agreed to come in mainly for the record, and that his heart wasn't really in it. He came for two sessions and then dropped out. He also moved out and hired a lawyer. In that short time I could only get a sketchy impression of the marriage and what had gone wrong. One of the major problems that Jim identified was his frustration with Nancy's "low sex drive."

Unfortunately we never did get to work on their sexual relationship, because Jim went through with the divorce. In individual therapy sessions later on, however, Nancy owned up to the fact that sex had not been great, and that she was the one who had been saying no for years. She was feeling guilty and remorseful about that now. I told her that bad sex, like a bad marriage, wasn't all one person's fault. She probably had contributed to a bad situation, though, by not asserting herself, and by not trying to get what she wanted out of her marriage, from handling finances to making love. Instead of confronting these issues, she consistently avoided them. She felt one-down to Jim, and she acted that way. One consequence had been that she felt resentful and got turned off to sex.

Nancy was one of two children, and the only daughter of a loving but weak sort of man and a dominating but insecure and jealous mother. Even in its best moments, the atmosphere in her home had been thick with tension. Criticism and complaints abounded. Her mother was a truly difficult woman, and she dominated the household. It was a great irony, I thought, that it was Nancy who was labeled as "nasty," since from what I could gather that word seemed to describe her mother much better.

Events took a bad turn in Nancy's life when her younger sister, her mother's favorite, took ill and died suddenly. Nancy was in her preteens at the time, and she took it hard. As jealous siblings sometimes will, she felt guilty, as though she secretly believed that somehow she had caused her sister's death. She never shared this guilt with anyone, until she shared it with me some thirty years later.

Adolescence for Nancy was one long period of unending demands from her mother, which led in turn to unending fights. Her hidden guilt set Nancy up to believe it when her mother would call her selfish and uncaring. Then her mother came up with the nickname, "Nasty Nancy." That could bring Nancy to tears, and her mother used it often as a last resort in arguments.

Nancy's problems of self-esteem were fairly severe, and I would be oversimplifying it if I suggested that they were resolved by any one technique. I believe that her cure really began that day when she shared her long-held secret guilt with me. That was the start of a new perspective for Nancy, on her family, on growing up, and on herself.

Somewhere along the way in our work together, Nancy and I more or less stumbled on a technique that helped her not slip back into childhood ways of thinking about herself. Once we got "Nasty Nancy" out into the open, I asked Nancy to try keeping track of situations in which this image came to mind. In particular, I asked her to remember the times when she felt like "the person with the nasty insides," as her mother had often said. Those were times, I said, when her self-esteem would be lowest. They would be situations where she would feel guilty and ashamed, one-down and unable to stand up for herself. She said that was right—that was exactly the way she had always felt when her mother called her that name.

The image of "Nasty Nancy" had caused Nancy a lot of trouble over the years. First with her husband, and later on with her two sons, she had a hard time saying no. She rarely stood up to a challenge to her authority, or negotiated for what she wanted. She recounted example after example of times when she backed off and gave in instead of standing her ground, sacrificed what she wanted instead of trying for a compromise.

Then one day Nancy came in and told me that she had a confrontation with her teenage son over the car they shared now that Jim had moved out. The boy wanted the car so he could go out with his girlfriend; Nancy needed it to do some shopping. She put her foot down, and her son stormed out of the house. I asked her how she felt about it.

"To tell you the truth," said Nancy, "it's the first time I can recall doing something like that. And I'll have to admit, it felt uncomfortable. I didn't like fighting with him. I felt scared. I don't know why I should be afraid of my own son, but I was. I was afraid of putting my will up against his, I suppose. I wasn't sure I'd come out on top. I also felt bad saying no, even though it was perfectly obvious that what I needed the car for was a lot more important than what he wanted it for. I found myself feeling like Nasty Nancy again there for a minute, and that's when I was close to giving in. But I held my ground."

"How were you able to hold your ground?" I asked. "What enabled you to resist the Nasty Nancy image instead of giving in to it?"

"Well, actually," Nancy replied, "the funniest thing happened. At one point in our conversation—in our fight I should say—I just happened to be standing by a wall in our family room. We have a lot of family pictures on that wall, including one of me when I was about eight or nine. I remember it because it was taken not too long after my sister died. I never liked that picture, probably because it brought back bad memories. Anyway, my son and I were going at it, and I looked at that picture, and all of a sudden I could hear my mother calling me Nasty Nancy again. It made me mad. 'No I'm not!' I said in my head. 'That's just something you made up to intimidate me, so you could get your own way!' And then the feeling, that bad feeling in the pit of my stomach, went away. And then I said no to my son and he stormed out of the house."

Nancy laughed, and it was obvious she was pleased with herself. For my part, I was impressed by the effect that looking at that picture had and on the way it enabled Nancy to stick to her guns and resist backing down. It was more or less both of our ideas to give Nasty Nancy a special place in Nancy's life after that. She had two copies made of that picture. She tacked one up in the kitchen; she kept the other one on her desk at work. From then on, whenever Nancy found herself at odds about how to act in a situation, torn between a desire to give in versus a desire to stand up for herself, she looked at that picture first.

It worked like a charm. It really was amazing how much that picture helped Nancy to change. It brought things into perspective, and it gave her that little extra boost she needed to stand her ground instead of running away.

Maybe you have a poor image of yourself, too, one that's rooted in a past that is still haunting you, still standing in your way. Think about Nancy's discovery, and how it might work for you. Get hold of some old photo albums, and pick out one picture that captures you at an age where you felt bad about yourself. Keep that picture handy. Take it out and look at it whenever you feel yourself about to give in when you know you ought to fight, when you want to give up when your heart tells you to press on. Think: Am I still the person in that picture? Can I be different now? Do I have to act like that person, give in to that old image, or can I do something else? Do I have a choice?

It worked for Nancy, and it can work for you, too.

Setting Limits

Self-esteem is something that can be developed, much the same way that physical fitness can be developed. We can get stronger, physically and psychologically, through the right kinds of exercise.

What kinds of exercise build self-esteem? There are two things in particular that do this: *setting limits,* and *setting priorities.* When we learn to say no, and when we learn to make choices on the basis of priorities, we build self-esteem. Let's look first at limits.

❦   ❦   ❦

Jim was basically a gentle person, but he often put people off because of his abrasive, aggressive style of talking. Hidden beneath this tough exterior, though, was an incredibly soft center, along with some severe problems of self-esteem. The roots of his self-doubts weren't hard to understand.

As a child Jim had been sickly to the point where he frequently had to spend weeks at a time in bed. He missed a lot of school, and though he was bright his grades were spotty. He had few friends, and was often picked on by stronger boys. He was more or less the class goat, and got more than his fair share of teasing. To cap things off, instead of giving him that extra bit of love, support, and attention that a sickly child typically needs, the rest of his family more or less ignored Jim.

As an adult, Jim looked back on his childhood with bitterness. He was angry at everyone, but in particular he was angry at his father for letting him down.

"How did he do that?" I asked.

"By being weak instead of strong," Jim replied. "By always giving in instead of fighting."

What young Jim had wanted was a strong father, a model he could look up to. He wanted someone who would stick up for him; someone who would defend his interests inside the family and out in the world. He wanted a father who would want to be pals even with a sickly son. But Jim's father was quiet and aloof, a man who kept to himself and pretty much let his wife and three daughters have the run of the house, while he lost himself in work and television.

When he came to see me, Jim's main complaint was about his girlfriend Sarah. There were problems in their relationship, he explained, but the thing that was bothering him the most was that Sarah had recently told him that she wanted to date other men. At the same time, she didn't want to have sex with Jim any more.

By itself, Sarah's desire to date around wasn't anything unusual. That kind of thing happens all the time. It hurts to be on the receiving end of that news, but let's face it, lots of people make those kinds of decisions. What made it unusual in this case was the rest of the story. It seemed that, even though he didn't live with Sarah, for the past two years Jim had been paying the rent on her apartment. He also paid the utility bills, and gave her money each week for food and gas. Lately she'd been asking for more money.

"Why does she want *more* money?" I asked.

"Because she needs new clothes," Jim explained, "and a new car."

"You mean," I asked, feeling my stomach twitch, "that Sarah is asking you for more money at the same time that she's telling you she wants to date around? At the same time she's saying she doesn't want to be sexually involved with you, she's asking you to help pay for new clothes?"

"That's right," said Jim.

"How do you feel about that? Do you think it might be a little unreasonable?"

"Not really," Jim replied. "I can understand why she needs the clothes, especially if she wants to date. And her car's getting pretty old."

"Do you think maybe you should say no?"

"I don't see where that would get me," he replied. "Then she probably wouldn't want to see me at all."

I couldn't believe it or didn't want to. Was this man really willing to go this far? Did he have no self-respect? How could he pay for clothes that Sarah would wear on dates with other men?

The more we talked, the more I could feel my blood starting to boil. I was getting angry at Jim. No matter what I said, or how I approached it, I could see that he wasn't going to be willing to say no to Sarah. He just didn't have the confidence to set any limits in the relationship. Just like his father, who had abdicated all influence to his wife and daughters, Jim would give in to Sarah, no matter how unreasonable her demands might be, even if it meant having to work two jobs to pay for the things she wanted.

I was surprised at how hard Jim resisted understanding what

I meant when I kept telling him that he was keeping himself down by not being able to say no to Sarah. When I'd question his decisions, he'd get angry, accuse me of meddling, of trying to break them up. This went on for months. Finally, in a fit of exasperation, I threw up my hands and got my feelings off my chest. "I'm tired," I said, " of sitting here and listening to you rationalize away all common sense. You accuse me of trying to break up your relationship, but to tell you the truth I don't see where it's a relationship at all. All you're doing is avoiding reality by refusing to set any limits. You're hoping that by doing that you'll keep Sarah. But you're kidding yourself. What's really happening is that you're giving away any shred of respect she might possibly have for you. Your self-esteem is already low, and the way you're acting will keep it there. Unless you face up to that, you're never going to get anywhere."

I figured that my little outburst probably wrecked my relationship with Jim. I felt bad. I figured he wouldn't show up for our next appointment. But I was wrong. I was pleased when he came back the next week, and even more pleased when he told me that he thought about what I had said. Maybe I had a point. Maybe he did need to build up his self-esteem. Maybe that's what turned off Sarah. Maybe what she was looking for was a stronger, more self-confident man.

I told Jim I wasn't sure that building his self-esteem would get Sarah back, but I thought it was something we ought to work on anyway. I also explained that he couldn't do that simply by talking to me.

"What do you mean?" he asked.

"I mean, you're going to have to *do* things," I replied.

"Like what?" he asked, cautiously.

"Like setting limits," I replied, " and making choices. You're going to have to decide how far you're willing to go, and be willing to take a stand. Building self-esteem requires exercising your willpower. You'll have to *work* your way to a better self-image. Just like you work your way to physical fitness."

The best way to learn to set limits is to learn to say *no*. Use this exercise to help you learn to do this.

Step 1: To begin, put yourself in a room by yourself. Close the door, and practice saying no. Say it *out loud*. Try saying it different ways: forcefully, gently, with a laugh in your voice, with anger in your voice.

This exercise may sound silly, but it works. Jim did it, once a day, for a month. At first he did it shyly. He told me how he stood in the middle of his bedroom, saying "no" in low tones. I asked him to demonstrate for me, in the office. He cleared his throat. "No?" he said. We worked on it for a while, until he was able to erase the question from his voice and make a clear statement.

Try this for yourself. Maybe you, too, will start out saying no very tentatively. Maybe, like Jim, you'll be asking a question, instead of making a statement. Work on making it into a statement, then a firm statement. Work your way up to being able to say it this way: "NO!"

As a final check, tape-record yourself saying no several times. Listen to the tape. Do you sound convincing?

Step 2: Once you've practiced saying no, and have gotten to the point where you can do it with force, as a statement, it's time to introduce a little fantasy into the exercise. Take a piece of paper and a pencil, and jot down three or four situations you remember when you think you should have said no, but didn't. For Jim, this wasn't hard to do. He rarely said no, but could think of lots of situations where he should have. For example, he knew he should have said no to Sarah's request for money for clothes. It wasn't hard for him to think of many other situations where he should have set a limit, but hadn't.

The next step was for Jim to imagine himself in those situations again, where he should have said no but didn't. For instance, he was to imagine the phone conversation where Sarah had asked him for extra money for clothes. He was to practice saying *no*, instead of yes, to her request. As with Step 1, he was supposed to do this *out loud*, and work on saying it in a firm tone of voice.

Do this exercise for yourself. After you've worked on saying no out loud and firmly, practice saying it out loud and

182

just as firmly in a situation you imagine. Let it be a real situation you were in: one where you should have set a limit but didn't.

Step 3: You can probably guess what this third and final step is: it's saying no—setting a limit—in some *real-life* situation. Jim did it, and you can, too. This is the hardest part of the exercise, but if you've followed through on the first two steps, you have the tools at hand to accomplish it.

It doesn't matter whether you start small or big, whether you set a limit over something relatively minor, or set it over some major issue. In fact, it's probably better to start small, if you can. The effect of setting limits is the same in both kinds of situations: it builds self-esteem and makes you feel equal instead of one-down.

Setting Priorities

Setting limits and establishing priorities are related. In Marge's case this connection was especially clear. She was involved for nearly three years with a man who lived in another city. While it was apparent that she was very serious about him, it was equally apparent from what she said that he wasn't so interested in her. He enjoyed her attention, and he wanted her to visit him. But her visits had to be worked around his busy work schedule. To accommodate him, Marge's plans frequently had to be changed at the last minute. Either David would ask her to come down after she had already made other plans, or he would call to cancel, saying he had work to do.

All in all I thought David's behavior revealed a more or less self-centered attitude, and I said so. To an extent, Marge agreed. "He can be kind of self-absorbed at times," she said, "But then, he has a very demanding position. I figure, to make a relationship work with a man like David, you have to compromise. I can't expect things to always go my way. That would be selfish."

"I agree," I said, "about compromising. But have you noticed that you seem to be the one doing almost all of the compromising in this relationship?" She didn't see it that way, so I backed off.

In addition to David, there were several other people in Marge's life who often placed unreasonable demands on her—in particular her parents, who were divorced but who both expected a lot in terms of time and attention. Marge was one of those people—those with low self-esteem—who are vulnerable to giving in, instead of setting limits. As a result they end up feeling bad about themselves, and depressed. They feel one-down in relationships, and sooner or later they start to hold back and withdraw.

Due to her difficulty in setting limits, a lot of people in Marge's life had developed the attitude that they came first. She didn't realize it, but she played a big role in spoiling them and making them so unreasonable. Marge always said yes, usually with a smile; but inside she resented the unreasonable demands of the people in her life. Though she rarely asked them outright for much, she resented them when they gave her very little. She couldn't turn down a request, but neither could she bring herself to make requests. She would drop what she was doing in an instant to do what someone else wanted, and later complain to me that she wasn't getting her own work accomplished. I told her she was making herself miserable.

In the midst of all her yes-saying, Marge's own goals and priorities got lost in the shuffle. For several years she'd been slowly working her way through college, taking one or two courses at night. She wanted to get out of secretarial work, and pursue a career in business. Her long-range goal was to get a master's degree and become an accountant. These were great plans, and until recently her grades were good enough to make them a real possibility. Lately, however, it seemed that she had lost all her motivation. She was depressed and had even contemplated quitting school.

Like Jim, Marge had big problems in the area of self-esteem. I told her that in order to build self-esteem she had to learn to set limits. That made her visibly uneasy. She also had to establish priorities and learn to make decisions based on those priorities. Judging by the decisions she made, she had two main priorities in life: David and her parents. Whatever else was going on, whatever else needed time or attention, she would drop in an instant to tend to them. That needed to change.

"The only way that you're going to get more out of life," I said, "including your relationships with David and your parents, is by learning to put yourself ahead of others at times. Maybe that seems ironic, but believe me it's true. To do that , though, you need to know what your priorities are. In other words, you need to know what *you* want. From what you've told me, two things you want very much are a college degree and a more fulfilling career. But you won't have either if you don't make them priorities and start making decisions based on those priorities."

Setting your own priorities can be difficult and frustrating if you're someone who always puts others first—who lets others set your priorities. If you're used to operating according to what someone else wants, getting in touch with what you want may not be easy. You'll need to persevere in order to do this.

The approach that worked for Marge was to think first about her goals and then about her priorities. The kind of lifestyle she eventually wanted was the key to understanding what her priorities needed to be in order to get there. We also talked about the kinds of things that made her feel good. Working together we came up with a list of things she liked to do for fun. Her list included things like cooking, sex, taking walks, and camping.

Come up with a list of things you like to do, things you want, and goals you have. If you're having trouble, think about where you would like to be ten years from now, and what you'll need to do in order to get there.

Once we had our lists, I had Marge rank the things on them, in groups, from those that were most important, to those that fell somewhere in the middle, to those that were relatively less important.

After you've made your list, go through it and organize the items into three groups: most important, important, and less important.

185

I explained to Marge that the result of this little exercise was a list of personal priorities. Now, I said, came the hard part, which was to learn to make decisions based on her priorities. I gave her two ground rules for doing this:

Ground Rule 1: Go over your list of personal priorities every day, and estimate how many got some attention that day, and how many got none.

Ground Rule 2: Make a decision, every day, about one priority that you'll give some time and attention to the next day.

Following these ground rules helped Marge make choices, and to begin to run her life according to her own priorities instead of others'. Since she couldn't do everything, she'd sometimes have to choose one priority over others to be given some special attention. Sometimes she would even have to choose herself over others.

As you might expect, at first this exercise was very difficult for Marge. I explained to her that it was indeed "exercise"—only this kind of exercise was building self-esteem instead of muscles. In both cases, though, the exercise was hardest at first. With practice, I assured her, it would get easier.

Sure enough, it did get easier, and it will for you, too. The more you exercise, the stronger you'll get. Your self-esteem will start to grow with the very first decision, the very first *choice* you make based on your own priorities. And it will continue to grow every time you do this.

Asserting Yourself

Setting limits and establishing priorities relates very much to what's popularly known these days as *assertiveness*. Assertiveness can be thought of as another tool for building self-esteem. Assertiveness boils down to *communication*. Being assertive means being able to communicate clearly your real feelings, thoughts, desires, and opinions. In contrast, unassertive people don't communicate these things very often, or very clearly.

Being assertive means being able to communicate positive feelings just as much as it involves learning to express negative ones. You can get just as far with praise as you can with criticism.

A person can have trouble expressing positive feelings, negative feelings, or both. Learning to be *positively assertive* means learning to be able to say things like:

- *I want . . .*
- *I'd like it if you . . .*
- *I like you.*
- *That feels good.*
- *Thank you.*

On the other hand, learning to be *negatively assertive* also has its place in life. It means being able to say things like the following:

- *Please stop that.*
- *Why are you late?*
- *I don't want . . .*
- *I'm not interested.*
- *I can't.*
- *That makes me mad.*
- *I don't like that.*

Do you find yourself making statements like these in the course of everyday living? Is there room in your important relationships for words like these? If you can't say things like this to someone you're close to, then maybe you should look at how close you feel to them. Relationships that lack assertiveness often also lack closeness, and sexual interest, too. Intimacy and passion, it seems, simply can't survive in relationships that don't have room for the expression of feelings. That includes positive feelings *and* negative feelings.

Being Assertive

You can learn to be more assertive by following the same rules that were described earlier for learning to say no. Learning to say no, after all, is only one example of using assertiveness as a tool for building self-esteem. In that case, it helps you set a limit.

To build self-esteem you need to go further than just setting limits. You can do this by applying the basic three-step method described earlier to *any* of the above assertive statements (as well as to any others you might think of). This process, again, goes like this:

Step 1: Spend some time alone, two or three times a week, and practice saying *out loud* an assertive statement. Concentrate on how your voice sounds, and work toward making a clear, firm statement. Be sure to practice positive *and* negative assertive statements. Tape-record yourself to make sure that you express yourself clearly and convincingly.

Step 2: Imagine some situations where you *could have* made an assertive statement but didn't. In private again, practice making assertive statements out loud while you imagine yourself being in those situations. Practice both positive and negative assertiveness.

Step 3: Extend your exercise into *real* situations. Begin to use the statements you've practiced with in private in your day-to-day life. Start small at first, using positive and negative assertions that don't make you faint with anxiety. Choose situations where your assertiveness is most likely to succeed, with the least chance of negative consequences. Try complimenting someone, for example, or asking for something simple. Disagree with someone over something minor, or express affection and appreciation to someone you're close to.

The more you "exercise," the stronger your self-esteem will get. Remember, though, like any exercise program, you

---

need to start out at a level you can handle and gradually work your way up. Also, remember the weight lifter's motto: *No Pain, No Gain*. Sometimes we have to take a risk, push ourselves to the limit, if we want to get stronger.

10

Trust

In the last chapter we looked at the role that self-esteem plays in staying in love. Intimacy depends on being open and honest, but to be open and honest it's essential that we feel that we're on an equal footing with the person we want to be intimate with. Otherwise, if we feel one-down, the vulnerability of intimacy will be too threatening.

One of the factors that's critical to feeling equal is self-esteem. What is self-esteem? It's a solid sense of who we are, of our boundaries and our priorities. It's a sense of confidence in our ability to pursue goals, confront issues, and take care of ourselves. Self-esteem leads to feelings of personal worth and self-respect. To a person with low self-esteem, the prospect of getting close and being open may seem more like a threat than an opportunity. They're apt to fear that they may lose rather than expand themselves through an intimate involvement. The person with low self-esteem stays hidden, which is the opposite of being intimate.

Self-esteem is one cornerstone in the foundation that we need in order to experience intimacy and maintain sexual desire in long-term relationships. In this chapter we'll look at the second cornerstone of this foundation, which is trust. Intimacy and sexual desire alike are deeply affected when we are unable to trust. The more we can trust, the more we can open up, emotionally, sexually, in every way. On the other hand, the less we trust the more we'll hold back.

Trust, Intimacy, and Sexuality

Nothing can do more to hurt a relationship than a breakdown in trust. Without trust there can be no openness; and when trust fails, so usually does sexual desire. Nothing has revealed this more dramatically than the research that's been done in the past decade on the effects of child abuse.

Boys as well as girls can be the victims of abuse, sexually and physically, and it's probably safe to assume that the effects are similar. In terms of hard facts, though, we know more about what abuse, and particularly sexual abuse, does to girls, and its later effects on them as women. Let's look at some of those facts.

Studies have shown that the lasting effects of abuse can include anxiety attacks, chronically disturbed sleep, recurring nightmares, depression, eating disorders, and stress-related physical illnesses such as ulcers and migraine headaches. Many nagging physical ailments that were once thought to be "hysterical," including headaches, stomach problems, fainting, and dizziness, can plague victims of abuse for years afterward.

Equally important are the long-term effects of abuse on victims' ability to be intimate and on their sexuality. Well over half the women who were victims of abuse as children report having severe fears of men as adults. Nearly half of these women never marry, and those who do are likely to marry men who have violent tempers, and therefore end up in relationships that repeat the earlier pattern of abuse. Nearly three out of four suffer from sexual dysfunctions that are caused by their inability to relax and get aroused. Not surprisingly, they suffer from low self-esteem, have poor body images, and low sex drives.

Abuse can be overt and physical, or it can be indirect and psychological. The girl who is molested, the boy who is beaten, are victims to be sure. But what about the girl who is subjected to constant criticism, or the boy who is belittled for all of his faults and flaws? They, too, may be vulnerable to the problems that haunt the adult lives of those who were more overtly abused as children. Abuse is abuse, and its common denominator is that it destroys trust and undermines self-esteem. Distrust creates alienation and stands as an obstacle to intimacy. To be able to be open, and to let yourself experience sexual passion, you must be able to trust.

The Roots of Distrust

"I was married for six months when I was twenty. Looking back on it, I think I got married just because I wanted to be married. I think I was afraid of being alone. It was a big mistake. We didn't really get along that well when we dated, and it beats me why I picked him to marry. It only got worse, until one day he hit me, and that was it. When he got home from work that day, I was gone.

"After that I had a lot of boyfriends, but they never lasted very long. Most of the time it was me who broke it off. I didn't feel close anymore after a while. I usually found myself getting edgy, and less interested in sex, too. That bothered them a lot, especially since early in a relationship I'm usually very sexual. I don't know how I got into that pattern. I wonder if it's something in me, like I'm afraid to get too involved. Sometimes it feels that way: that I start backing away just as soon as things start getting close.

"Jerry and I have been together almost three years now. It's the longest relationship for me ever. He wants to get married, but I know I'm afraid of that. In the last year, our sex life has started to deteriorate, and I know it's me who's to blame. I'm the one who's losing interest. It's my old pattern again. He isn't any different than he used to be, and I used to like making love with him.

"I'm not very good at arguing. I can defend myself up to a point. But as soon as he raises his voice, I go to pieces. I give up. I stop fighting, and the argument ends. But I think maybe there's something left over, because I definitely want to get away from him then, and I definitely don't want to have sex. Twice now, after we've argued about something minor over the phone, I haven't gone home that night. That drove him up the wall. Most of the time I can't even remember the things I'm mad about, but I must be mad, because when Jerry comes on to me I often feel angry inside."

"When we were first married I threw myself into my relationship with Herb. I was about as totally open with my feelings as I can imagine anybody being. I was crazy about him. I came on to him all the time. But he let me down so many times that now I feel totally closed off to him. To be honest I don't know what he could do to get me to open up again, to really trust him again. I don't want to have sex with him; I don't even want him to touch me now."

Two instances of distrust: one rooted in the past, the other in the present. Vicky, the first woman, had an abusive, alcoholic father who'd abandoned his family when she was about eight, after doing a lot of damage. It left her with an abiding distrust and fear of men. It prejudiced her and had turned her own relationships into self-fulfilling prophecies of frustration and failure. Her marriage only served to confirm what she had learned as a child: that you can't count on, or be safe around, a man. With Vicky, men didn't stand a chance. She was ready to reject them from the start, and she was always looking for reasons to justify her basic desire to run away. She had no faith in love, because she had never been loved.

Mary, the second woman, had married a man who was so self-centered and immature that he could never allow himself to be tied down by even the most minor of commitments. Asking Herb to make a promise, no matter how small, and live up to it, was like asking for his right arm. It was inviting disappointment. He proved and reproved this until Mary finally saw the light and left him.

In both of these women, distrust was at the root of the problems they were having feeling close or sexual with their partners. In one case the present distrust was warranted, while in the other it was more or less a carryover from the past. In Vicky's case the problem was solved through confronting the past and getting control over it. Vicky needed to stop allowing the past to control the present. She needed to take a risk and try judging just one man on the basis of his own behaviour, instead of stereotyping him because of her experiences with her father. She lumped all men together and failed to see them as individuals. In some ways, I thought, she baited them, trying to get them angry so that she could "expose" their cruelty and abusiveness. What she needed was to find a little faith.

In Mary's case the issue was just the opposite. She needed to learn to trust her own instincts, instead of being talked out of them, and to judge a person by his actions as much as by his words. Once she did this, she could see her partner as he really was, and make a decision. She could stop blaming herself for being "frigid," and start looking at how her partner's behavior was turning her off.

Two final examples will give you a good sense of how distrust relates to problems of intimacy and sexual desire. Then we can talk about what you might be able to do about it if you are caught in a web of distrust. The first is a woman whom we can call Debbie. She and her partner Tom came to therapy at his insistence because of her loss of sexual desire. The problem had been going on for over a year, but things had become a lot worse in the past six months. Tom was at the point where he was having second thoughts about marrying Debbie; meanwhile, she was feeling very guilty about being so turned off to sex.

"I just don't seem to have a sex drive any more," said Debbie. "I'm never interested. I never even have sexy dreams any more. Do you think that's just the way I am? Are there some people who just lose their drive for sex?"

The problem that accounted for Debbie's loss of sexual desire wasn't in her hormones, but in her relationship with Tom. Over the year or so before they came to see me, she had gradually developed a strong distrust of him. As it turned out, Debbie was not even aware of the extent of her distrust. I became aware of it, though, as I watched her and Tom interact in my office, and as I listened to their accounts of what went on at home between sessions.

In our sessions Tom presented himself as the "normal" one in the relationship. He wanted to get close to Debbie, he said, but found her rejecting and cold. He attributed this to her family, which he described as cold and unaffectionate. "They're a bunch of cold fish," he said, "and she's just like them."

Debbie sat upright, looking angry. "Ever since I told him that my family wasn't as affectionate as his, he's been throwing it in my face. But I don't think it's all my fault, or all my family's fault, for that matter. There's got to be more to it than that."

Tom pressed her—actually, he more or less grilled her—to come up with the "something more." The more he pressured her, the more I saw Debbie withdraw. She got quiet, and she sank down into her chair.

I observed this same pattern many times in our sessions. Although Tom came on strong, and tended from my perspective to be overbearing and aggressive, he complained that Debbie wouldn't talk to him. From his perspective, her withdrawal was a problem in *her*. It had nothing to do, as far as he could see, with the way he came on. I could see how it did, though. He was very open in expressing his sexual frustration, and wondered aloud what could be wrong with Debbie. "I don't understand," he'd say, "why she doesn't have the same sexual needs as every other woman I've known."

The fact was that Debbie had not "lost" her sex drive. She had *turned off*. I told her she probably had as strong a sex drive as she ever did, but that it was being blocked by something. To discover what that might be, I suggested that she and Tom could try doing something physical together, like a sensual massage. Tom was enthusiastic. Debbie agreed reluctantly to try it.

A week later I found Debbie sitting alone in my waiting room. Tom, she said, had refused to come in. He was angry, and was threatening to leave. "What happened?" I asked. "Did you follow through on what we agreed?"

They had tried the massage all right, Debbie explained, and things had actually gone very well up to a certain point.

"What point?" I asked.

"Up until I thought it was time to stop. But Tom didn't. Apparently he thought we were going to have sex. I said no."

"What happened then?"

"He blew up. He flew off the handle. He yelled and shouted, called me every name in the book. Actually, I'm getting tired of that. Whenever he gets mad he drags everything he can think of out of the closet and clobbers me with it. Everything I ever told him in confidence gets thrown in my face. Then he complains that I don't talk to him!"

I told Debbie that I could understand Tom's frustration. No one likes to be on the receiving end of sexual rejection. I could even understand his getting mad. But the way he reacted also made me wonder how much Debbie's trust might have been undermined in this relationship.

"What do you mean?" she asked.

I asked Debbie to describe how she felt after one of Tom's outbursts, when he would hurl angry accusations and use things said in confidence against her.

"Like I said—clobbered. I feel beaten up," she said. "I feel *emotionally* beaten, and I don't think I can take it much longer. It's even worse if he's been drinking. I've told him that, but he won't listen.''

It was pretty clear to me that Tom's verbal assaults were driving Debbie away. The more often it happened—the more often he lost control and lashed out viciously—the less Debbie could feel safe with him. I thought he had created his own situation, for this tendency to lash out had been there from the start of his relationship with Debbie, when sex between them had been good.

Paul and Ginny came in for help with his low sexual desire. In taking a history I learned that the problem went deeper than sex. Ginny felt that Paul held back a lot, and that he resisted getting close to her in every way, not just sexually. In the two years they had lived together he never sent Ginny a birthday card, a Valentine's card, even a romantic note. He never bought her presents, never said he loved her, and was rarely physically affectionate. On the other hand, she explained, he didn't abuse her, physically or emotionally, like her husband and father both had. "He may hold back," she said, "but at least I don't have to worry about getting beaten up."

Paul and Ginny both had issues of trust. She had settled for a relationship that was not very fulfilling, but where she was in many ways the one in control. She earned most of the money, for instance, and it was her house that they lived in. Paul, meanwhile, was also one of the most distrustful persons I've ever met. And he held back in relationships more than almost anyone I've met. It was no wonder he had such severe difficulties with intimacy and sexual passion. He was close to militant when it came to maintaining separate spaces, and downright paranoid about getting hurt. He absolutely refused to make any sort of commitment to Ginny. Whenever she brought up the idea, he would literally disappear for two or three days. He always came back, but the message in his actions was clear: Don't try to tie me down.

Paul could certainly be cold and unloving, but under the right conditions he could be a little warm and affectionate. The key to this was that he could only be affectionate when he wasn't *asked* to be. As long as he could feel that he was acting completely voluntarily, he could be somewhat loving and affectionate. But that's how it had to be: absolutely no strings attached. Under those conditions he could get a little close. As soon as Paul felt the least pressure to do something, however, to get close or make a commitment, he could be counted on to do just the opposite. That's how I came to understand his never sending a Valentine, or a birthday card. To him, meeting social expectations felt like giving in to a demand. By the same token, buying a present on Ginny's birthday implied a commitment he was not willing to make.

Sex was the same story. So long as Ginny didn't *ask* for it, they could occasionally have sex—not at all frequently or regularly, but occasionally. And when they did make love, Ginny could get some satisfaction so long as she didn't *ask* Paul to do anything. As soon as she either asked to make love, or asked Paul to do something for her in bed, he turned off. "He literally acts like I turned some switch off. I've never met a man who can turn off his passion like that. It leaves me out in the cold. He won't talk about it, but it's as though he's saying, 'Take what's offered, or get nothing at all.' "

Why was Paul so distrustful? Because he, too, had been the victim of abuse. In his case it was his mother who had done a lot to undermine Paul's ability to trust. She apparently had severe emotional problems, problems that Paul never did understand to his satisfaction. She was unpredictable, and could violently attack anyone in the family, verbally or physically, without any clear provocation. As a result, Paul grew up in an atmosphere where it was best to be on guard. At eighteen he left, but by then his distrust had already been deeply ingrained.

With Debbie and Paul we have two more cases of distrust. In both cases their distrust was undermining their relationships, standing in the way of intimacy and sexual desire. The difference in their cases is that in one the distrust had its causes mainly in the present, while in the other the causes were mostly in the past. The distrust that Debbie had for Tom was deserved. He really did "beat" her emotionally. Paul's distrust, on the other hand, had little if anything to do with Ginny or the way she treated him.

Men (and women) like Paul look for reasons in the present to justify a distrust that has its real roots in the past. They have a basically distrusting attitude toward others, and take the position that others shouldn't be trusted unless they can prove themselves trustworthy. This places the burden of proof on others, keeps them on the defensive, and puts the distrustful person in the position of judging everyone else. Under those conditions it's hard for love to survive.

How can you tell if you, or your partner, may have a basically distrustful attitude that could be causing trouble in your relationship? Here are some of the signs:

- Do you tend to dig your heels in and say no when someone asks you to do something? Distrustful people are inclined to take the attitude that they'll be very helpful and cooperative so long as they do it voluntarily.
- Distrustful people are people whom you'd call "thin skinned." Their feelings get easily hurt, and they hold on to grudges.
- Do you feel that others let you down a lot? Distrustful people often think that way.
- Do you resent it when you have to ask your partner to do something for you? Do you feel that he or she should know enough to do it without having to be asked? Distrustful people often feel that if others cared more, they wouldn't have to ask for things.
- Distrustful people usually believe that others, including people close to them, take advantage of them. Do you believe that?

People like Debbie, who are basically trusting, have several advantages over people like Paul, who are distrustful. As a group they're happier. They're also more popular. They can get close

to others more easily, and generally speaking others are attracted to them. Like Debbie, they can *learn* to distrust, but they
don't begin relationships with that assumption.

People who've been abused in one way or another have good
reason to be distrustful. Still, their distrust prejudices them,
and they may not give someone else a fair chance. Has this been
true for you, or for someone you've tried to get close to?
Have you failed to show faith in someone you should have
trusted?

So far I've given you examples that illustrate two ways that
people can become distrustful. One way is to have been the victim of abuse as a child, or in other past relationships. That destroys trust and makes it difficult for the former victim to open
up to others later on.

The second way to become distrustful is through experience
in your current relationship. Like Debbie, we can learn to back
off from someone who continually lets us down, who betrays
our trust, or who abuses us in the here and now. That can also
cause problems later on, because once we learn to distrust it's a
hard habit to break.

There's a third way that people can become distrustful, which
doesn't have much to do with real experience, either in the past
or the present. That way is through *modelling*. The most
influential models we're exposed to are our parents. More than
we may want to admit, our own attitudes and values are
reflections of their attitudes and values.

Think back for a moment on your own childhood. Picture
those people who were most important in your life: your parents, other relatives who played a role in your upbringing,
teachers who made an impression on you. What do you think
their attitudes were about other people, and particularly about
trust? Which of the following statements would come closest to
what *they* would probably think?

- People shouldn't be trusted unless they can prove to you
  that they're trustworthy.

OR

- You're better off trusting someone unless you have some good reason to think otherwise.

- Most people can be counted on to be pretty honest.

   OR

- Most people are likely to cheat unless someone is watching them.

Trusting and distrusting attitudes are passed down across generations. In reading through these choices, it shouldn't be hard to figure out which answers reveal a trusting outlook and which ones reflect a distrustful attitude toward others. Advocates of both positions can argue their cases and justify their beliefs. The issue isn't so much which attitude is right, but what their implications are for the way you relate to others. How would you expect a distrustful person to approach relationships? Would they have faith, or would they be cynics? Would that person be open and revealing, or closed and guarded? Do you think they would be inclined to let others know what they're feeling, or would they keep their emotions on a tight rein? Would they be intimate people? Which attitude—trust or distrust—do you think would lend itself to revealing feelings, including sexually passionate feelings?

Overcoming Distrust

Distrust undermines intimacy, and in the long run it destroys sexual desire as well. To keep intimacy and passion alive and growing requires trust. At the same time, to trust another person, especially to trust them deeply, can be one of the most difficult things we can do, particularly if our trust has been violated by abuse or neglect. To overcome the trauma of abuse, and to open yourself up again, takes real courage. However, unless we can find ways to overcome distrust, and to open up enough to give intimacy a chance, we may never discover it. Unless we can

THE HEART OF LOVE

find ways to build trust, our passion might stay locked away inside us forever.

Distrust and cynicism always have their roots in some form of betrayal. In some way, at some time, the distrustful person was let down and deeply hurt by someone he or she loved. Much distrust has its roots in stressful and hostile relationships with parents. A child may have been abused, sexually, physically, or psychologically. These are obvious and flagrant forms of betrayal. But a parent can also abuse a child, and betray its trust, by failing to love it, by neglecting it, or by rejecting it. The parent who belittles a child, or who fails to provide encouragement and affection, is betraying that child just as surely as the parent who takes a stick to it. In both cases, the long-range effect is the same: a child who grows up to be a distrustful adult.

The process outlined on the following pages can be helpful in getting you started on overcoming distrust. It will give you direction and tools, but one thing it can't give you is the courage to confront distrust and overcome it. You have a choice. On the one hand, you can play it safe, and stay distrustful. In that case you will protect yourself, but you will also pay a price. That price will be love. That's right, *love*. It's difficult to keep love alive when you stay closed and keep your feelings to yourself. Distrustful people tend to do just that.

On the other hand, you can take a chance . . .

Step 1: Confronting Your Distrust

The first step in learning to overcome distrust is to face up to just how distrustful you are. Taking an honest personal inventory of your attitudes may give you an idea of how much distrust could be undermining intimacy in your relationship, or how much it could be blocking your sexual passion.

How distrustful are you? Having read up to this point, you should be able to answer that question pretty well. You can look back on your own experiences as a child and in adult relationships. You can compare your experiences to some of the cases discussed earlier. Try to get in touch with whether you've felt abused, physically, sexually, or emotionally. Keep in mind that abuse isn't always obvious, and that it can be verbal as well as physical. Neglect can be as harmful as a beating. Being humiliated can be as bad as being beaten up.

How can you tell if you were the victim of psychological abuse? Well, there may not have been any physical bruises to point to, but there surely were emotional ones. The key questions are: Have you ever *felt* "beaten" in some way? Have you ever felt betrayed by someone you loved very much? If so, when? What were the circumstances? Who left you feeling beaten or betrayed? How often did it happen? Do you think those experiences also left you feeling distrustful? Did they destroy your faith in love?

Look back on the important figures from your formative years. Think about *their* attitudes. This may give you an idea about how much you may have modeled a trusting (or a distrusting) attitude.

A personal inventory is a vital first step toward overcoming distrust. Unless and until you can own up to just how distrustful you might be, you'll very likely be confused as to what keeps you from getting close to others, or what stops you from letting go with your sexual passion. You may find yourself falling out of love, but never know why.

If you are distrustful, how do you justify it? List the reasons you have for not trusting other people in general. Then list your reasons for not trusting someone you're in a relationship with now. How many of these reasons have to do with *previous* experiences you've had, either as a child or an adult? How much of your justification is based on attitudes you picked up through *modeling*, as opposed to real experience? How much of your distrust is based on actual experiences of abuse or betrayal in *this* relationship?

Step 2: Healing Wounds

The goal in helping people to trust is not to teach them to trust blindly. I'd be the last one to say that it's a good idea to go on trusting someone in the face of good evidence that they'll use you, abuse you, or betray you. But when you approach every relationship from the outset with these kinds of expectations, you don't give them a chance. They're more or less doomed from the start. The other person doesn't have a chance to get close to you. Through your cynicism you've set the stage for a self-fulfilling prophecy of disappointment and alienation.

Instead of trusting blindly, the goal in overcoming distrust is to learn to give people and relationships a chance—to judge each relationship on its own merits, each person on the basis of your actual experiences with them, rather than on the basis of some outlook you modelled when you were young, or on the basis of your experiences with others. This has nothing to do with being naïve or gullible. It has to do with not jumping to conclusions. Before you can take that chance, though, you may need to clear the air and bury some bad feelings left over from the past. Until you can confront the past and work it through, you won't be able to leave it behind.

How can you "heal" old wounds? Is it possible, you might ask, to overcome the fear and distrust that abuse and betrayal create? Skepticism might be your first reaction to the very idea of "healing." Am I really suggesting that you can simply undo these effects?

I'm not exactly suggesting that. It would be naïve to think that the harm that abuse does can be undone in any simple way. What I am suggesting, though, is that it's possible to get past the distrust that an earlier betrayal created long enough to give trust and intimacy a chance to get a toehold in a relationship now. It's possible to work through the fears, the anger, and the bitterness enough to give your love and sexual passion a chance to express themselves. One way to do this is to confront, instead of trying to avoid, the memories that drive your distrust. If you can do that, you can begin to conquer distrust. Let me give you an example to illustrate how this can work.

Several years ago I happened to be working with a very bright and sensitive woman psychologist. We were seeing a case together. It was a couple, and we were seeing them because the woman, Jane, was preorgasmic; in other words, Jane had never had an orgasm. We were approaching the midway point in therapy. Up to then our efforts had been focused mainly on what Jane could do for herself. Things had been moving along pretty well. As soon as we tried to get her husband involved, though, to start having them do things *together*, we suddenly found ourselves bogged down. Week after week our suggestions were avoided. Week after week we had to listen to excuses for why the things they agreed to do the week before hadn't been done. The excuses were always hers, and they were always lame. Pretty soon, both Jane's husband, Mike, and we were feeling exasperated. My co-therapist, Nan, suggested we meet individually with both partners to try to get a handle on what was going wrong.

During her session with us, Jane revealed that she had bad feelings—she described it as a "creepy" feeling all over her body— whenever Mike tried to touch her. From Mike we learned that this was nothing new; he often felt Jane stiffen up and pull back when he tried to touch her. But Jane was also having some disturbing nightmares, which she could never remember the next day, and twice she had woken up in the middle of the night in a cold sweat. Mike said this had never happened before.

We tried to help Jane identify what it was that had brought this on, but Jane could think of nothing. Then Mike mentioned the movie they had seen a couple of weeks earlier. The movie had included a graphic rape scene, and Mike thought Jane had acted very scared afterward.

Nan said that she saw the movie, too. She agreed that the

rape scene had been frightening. She asked Jane what she had thought of it. Was Mike right? Had it scared her?

"No," said Jane flatly. "I didn't have much of a reaction at all. Mike did, though. He said men like that ought to be castrated."

While she was speaking, I noticed that Jane's face had turned pale, and that her eyes had a glazed look about them. I looked at Nan and could tell that she noticed the same thing. When Jane stopped, Nan very gently asked her a question.

"Jane, can you remember if you were ever touched in a sexual way that made you scared or uncomfortable?"

Jane's face kept its stony appearance. There wasn't a trace of emotion in it. It was almost as though she was in a trance. It made me very uneasy. "No," she said weakly.

I wasn't convinced, and I sensed that neither was Nan, but we dropped the subject for the moment.

Two days later we got an urgent call from Mike. Jane was freaking out, he said. He couldn't think of anyone else to call, so he called us. Could he bring her in? Yes, we said, bring her in right away.

The first phase in Jane's recovery from the effects of what turned out to be childhood sexual abuse was for her to be able to confront the pain, the fright, and the shame that she had been keeping inside for many years. She had done such a good job of keeping a lid on her feelings that she even managed to hide them from herself for a long time. It seemed, though, that the combination of sex therapy, the movie, and Nan's question had been enough to crack the dam. Now Jane was being flooded with frightening emotions. She needed to vent those feelings, to unburden herself. To do this, however, she also needed to trust someone enough to be that vulnerable with. It turned out that Nan was the one person she had that trust in.

The trust that Jane had in Nan was the first real trust she'd felt in her life, and it enabled her to take the leap that was necessary in order for her to begin healing. I witnessed some of this, and I was deeply touched by what I saw. There was a lot of pain there; a lot of loneliness, too. The victim of abuse feels alienated from the rest of the world, alone with his or her shame and despair. Whatever betrayal they suffered causes a distrust that separates them from others.

Getting the bad feelings out took some time. Most of this work was done by Nan. Meanwhile, I worked with Mike. I tried to discover what he knew, without revealing his wife's secret before she was ready to tell him herself. I discovered what I suspected: that he didn't know anything at all. I tried to offer comfort and support while we bided our time until Nan felt we could move on as a team again.

Unburdening herself of all the pent up-feelings, facing the pain and fright and sharing it with someone else, proved to be immensely helpful to Jane. It marked the beginning of a recovery process that eventually enabled her to take some risks with Mike. Those risks were essential if she was going to see if intimacy was possible between them, and if she would ever be able to let herself go sexually. If she could open herself up without being betrayed, her relationship with Mike might grow, and they might just stay in love for the rest of their lives.

You might think that Jane's distrust was especially severe, and that the extent of her betrayal was unusual. But the truth is that her case is not that unusual, and that her distrust was not so exceptional. If you are distrustful, you may have felt every bit as betrayed, for your own reasons, as Jane was as a result of her sexual abuse.

To begin the process of healing, you need to be able to *share* your grief and sorrow, your anxiety and guilt. Some people choose to do this with a therapist, and that's fine. Therapy is as good a place as any to take a chance on trust. Ultimately, though, you need to be able to share your pain with someone you love. Whatever the cause of your distrust—no matter who betrayed you, or how—think about *sharing* it sometime, with someone close to you. The healing that this can do is the second vital step in overcoming distrust.

Step 3: Remodelling Your Attitudes

Remodelling is a process that consists of two phases. First, you need to take responsibility for attitudes that you've adopted, either as a result of a personal experience or through copying someone else's attitudes. These are beliefs that *you* hold primarily because someone else who was important to you also held them. You don't necessarily know *why* that other person held those attitudes - whether, for example, they had been abused.

Once you've taken responsibility for your attitudes, you also need to take responsibility for choosing either to keep them or to change them. Choosing to change means being willing to take a chance on outlooks that may be different from ones you have more or less copied. It means taking a chance on judging new relationships and new people on their own merits, rather than judging them against old relationships. It means being willing to withhold judgement long enough to see whether you can get close and still feel safe.

Think about your expectations for those who are closest to you. Do you feel that you are quick to judge, quick to feel let down by them? Do you tend to look for reasons to justify your distrust? Do you think you might be inclined to exaggerate the significance of normal human weaknesses, so that you feel betrayed over relatively minor incidents? Where in your past could this sensitivity, this readiness to feel betrayed, be coming from?

To be able to be intimate, you need to take responsibility for any tendency you may have to judge other people too harshly, to feel deeply hurt and betrayed over minor incidents, and to expect others to be more than human. These are all ways you can use to justify your distrust, keep others at a distance, and hold yourself back from being open.

Once you're in touch with your attitudes, have an idea of where they came from, and are willing to take responsibility for them, you're in a position to do something about them. You can see, for example, that your attitudes are not the result of genetics. You weren't *born* with a distrustful attitude, but either learned it directly or modelled it. The same is true for all of your other attitudes. And because they aren't ingrained in your genes, attitudes can be changed. You have the power of *choice*. As soon as you take responsibility for your attitudes, you'll realize that you have the power to try on *different* ones.

Trying on a different attitude, like trust instead of distrust, is not that difficult once you realize you can do it, and once you decide to do it. Try thinking of an attitude as a suit of clothes. Basically, it's something you have the choice to put on or take off, to keep or change. In many ways, the adage about how "clothes make the man" applies here. In a sense, attitudes make the person. The person who is trusting not only sees the world differently, but is seen differently by the world. People who are trusting act differently and are treated differently by others. If you doubt this at all, I challenge you to try an experiment in remodelling your attitudes. It involves trying on a trusting "suit of clothes."

Trying on a trusting suit of clothes boils down to taking the following attitude: *People are worth trusting unless you have some good reason to think otherwise.*

In other words, in your experiment with being a trusting person you must approach others and *start* relationships with the attitude that the other person can be counted on. If you do this, it will have a profound effect on the way you relate to others and on the way that others relate to you. Try it, and see for yourself.

People will be more open and friendly with you if you trust them. They'll want to be with you, and they'll feel more affectionate toward you. Intimacy becomes possible once you trust. People will open up to you, and you may find yourself opening up to them. Trust is the gateway to love. In contrast, distrust locks the door to love. Distrust breeds distrust. If you approach others with distrust, you put them on the defensive, and they'll distrust you. If you hold back from them, they'll hold back from you. Ironically, you'll feel rejected, but you've only created your own self-fulfilling prophecy.

Distrust that's rooted in the past can destroy a relationship that needs intimacy to grow in the present. If this seems to be the trouble in your relationship, why not take the chance on trying on a trusting attitude for a while? Yes, it can be scary, but it also could be the best "change of clothes" you've ever made in your life.

Building trust, like building self-esteem, takes "exercise." In both cases you need to be willing at some point to take a risk. Distrustful people feel very vulnerable, and that makes it hard for them to reveal themselves. Sooner or later, though, if you want to enjoy an intimate relationship, and if you want to be able to loosen up on the reins you keep your emotions under, you need to take that chance. You need to give your relationship a chance to grow in the here and now. The only way to do that is to let go of old experiences, just for a moment, and try being open and honest about what you think and feel.

Trusting is like putting yourself in another person's hands. If past experience has prejudiced you, so that you won't put yourself in your partner's hands for fear of being let down, then you're never going to feel as close to him or her as you possibly could. You will hold back, keeping your emotions in. On some level your partner will know this, and feel rejected by you. That destroys intimacy, and sooner or later sexual passion, too. And love without intimacy and passion is no love at all.

Think about it. The choice (and opportunity) is yours. You can play it safe and stay in your shell, or you can come out of your shell and see what the warm air and sunshine of intimacy feels like. You can hold on to old attitudes, or you can try on some new ones for size. You can keep the doors closed in your relationship, or open them up and see what lies on the other side.

PART V

Liberating
Passion and Intimacy

The sexual revolution was a struggle against sexual prejudice and ignorance. It was a fight for our right, as individuals, to be sexual. Today we face another struggle, only
this time it is couples who must work together to overcome
obstacles that undermine intimacy and sexual desire. Today's challenge is to make love last. In the final part of the
book we'll focus in on an issue that's been talked about a
lot here and that plays a key role in keeping intimacy and
passion alive and growing in a relationship. That's the issue of equality in relationships, and what it means for staying in love. ❦

11

Egalitarian Marriage

Chuck and Julie had been together for fifteen years, and married for twelve. Although they married young, they waited to have children until they both felt ready. That meant waiting until both of them felt that their careers were on a solid footing. Now they had two boys and a house. Julie hadn't worked while the children were babies, but now that they were in school she was back on a half-time basis.

As much as Julie had liked her time at home with her babies, she explained to me when we first met that she never felt totally comfortable about not having a job. Working had always given her a feeling of security. That feeling was definitely missing when she stayed at home. Not earning a salary made her feel one-down in relation to Chuck. "It's not as though he does anything to make me feel that way. It's more a feeling that I create. I guess deep down I must believe that money is power, and the person who doesn't have much money, doesn't have much power, either. No matter how nice he is—and Chuck *is* a nice person—I feel uneasy being financially dependent on him."

Chuck and Julie decided they needed therapy because, though

they agreed that their commitment to each other was sound, they also agreed that their sex life was in trouble. Chuck was becoming more and more upset over Julie's lack of interest in making love. It had started after their first son was born. Chuck noticed that Julie stopped initiating sex then, though she still responded when he made the first move. After their second son was born, she became increasingly unresponsive. At first she put him off gently, claiming to be too tired. But after a while, as Chuck found himself turned down more and more consistently and became irritable, Julie got angry and defensive. Pretty soon sex—and later on all physical affection—became a sore spot in their marriage. It was a subject they avoided as much as possible, until Chuck got so frustrated that he blew up, or Julie felt so guilty that she gave in.

"What bothers me most," said Chuck, "is that I don't feel Julie is even trying to make things better. If you want a good sex life—just like if you want a good career—I believe you need to put some effort into it. You can't just take it for granted and expect it to be good. I think I've put in a lot of effort. Frankly, I'd like to see her put something into it now."

I couldn't argue with Chuck's sentiments. I also believe that a good sex life needs effort and attention. It's not likely to grow if it's ignored or neglected. The same goes for intimacy. You won't feel close if you don't spend the time and put the energy into doing the things that make you feel close. But I needed to get Julie's perspective on things, too. What did she think the problem was? I was curious to see if there could be any connection between the feelings she said she had about being dependent on Chuck and her progressive lack of interest in sex after their children were born.

Julie agreed with Chuck that their sex life was in a slump. But she felt that it had had its ups and downs all along. The peaks and valleys admittedly seemed to have more to do with her changing interest than his. "I suppose it really is me who tends to run hot and cold," she said. "Still, I'm not sure that I agree with Chuck—that the answer is just *trying* harder. I mean, do people really have to *try* to have a sex life? Don't you think that making love should come naturally, without a lot of effort?"

"I suppose I agree and disagree," I replied. "I agree if what you're saying is that you shouldn't have to *force* yourself to have sex. Obviously, you should *want* to have sex. Faking an interest in sex never did anyone much good. On the other hand, I've seen too many couples who've simply given up. They've neglected their relationship and failed to nurture the *conditions* that lead to intimacy and sexual desire, and then they suffer the consequences. I think a good relationship, and a good sex life, requires commitment and work."

I turned to Chuck. "By the way," I asked, "what do you mean by *effort*? What is it you'd like Julie to do?"

"I'll give you an example," he replied. "Actually, this a another sore point between me and Julie, so we might as well get it out in the open right now." He sighed. I could see this was uncomfortable for him.

"I like to buy Julie things," he said.

"What kinds of things?" I asked.

Julie laughed, and Chuck frowned. "Go ahead, tell him," she said.

"Things to wear, like sexy underwear. Stuff that turns me on. Nothing kinky, just lacy, sexy-looking stuff. I don't think that's so unusual, do you? But she never wears them. I keep telling her that if it turns me on to see her in something like that, it could make her feel sexy just to wear it. But she won't even give it a try. I think she resents me for even suggesting it."

Chuck looked at me a bit sheepishly. "So, does that qualify me as a sexual pervert? Is there something wrong with me for wanting something different now and then?"

Julie broke in. "I don't think you're a pervert, Chuck. Really, I don't. It's just that, well, what's wrong with *me* the way I am? What's wrong with my body the way it is?"

Chuck sighed. I could tell they had been over this ground before. "There's nothing *wrong* with you," he said. "Sometimes I feel a little guilty saying that I'd like you to do something different, or wear something I buy you. I know you get the impression that that means I don't find you attractive the way you are, or like the way you make love. But that's not true. I *do* think you're attractive. And you're a fine lover. But I also think that a little diversity never hurts. It's like the saying goes, about having steak for dinner every night. No matter how good it is, sooner or later you'll get tired of steak. And sometimes I think maybe that's your problem, maybe you're bored with our sex life."

Julie frowned. "I know what you mean, but I can't help feeling the way I do. And I *do* wear the things you buy, Chuck. I just don't wear them as much as you'd like me to. And I've told you, maybe it turns you on, but it doesn't do much for me. Maybe it does bother me that you want me to wear those things. Maybe it makes me feel put down. Anyway, you may be bored, but I don't think that boredom is my problem. I know you probably don't believe it, but I find you as physically attractive as I ever did. But I also feel like I have to keep some distance. I can't explain it; it's just a feeling I have . . ."

"Of being on guard?" I interjected. "Just a little careful and defensive around Chuck?"

"Yes!" said Julie. "That's it! I think I *do* feel defensive and guarded. How did you know that? And *why* should I feel that way? He's never given me reason to feel that way. Chuck is a very considerate man. So why do I feel distant from him?"

"I'm thinking," I said, "about what you told me before, about how you've felt uncomfortable being financially dependent on Chuck. You said you still feel some of that. And if I heard you right, both your feeling of uneasiness and your loss of interest in sex started around the same time, after your first son was born and you stopped working."

Chuck and Julie's situation was not unusual. You may have been there yourself. I could sympathize with both of them, because in their own ways, and from their own perspectives, each of them was right. Chuck was saying, in effect, that it can be fun and exciting to spice up a sexual relationship now and then.

Julie was saying that she felt a need to keep a distance between her and Chuck, and that this feeling had started after she became financially dependent on him. For Chuck, keeping sexual interest alive took effort and creativity. He was right about that. But Julie's issue was on a different level altogether. If she had felt on an even footing with Chuck, his ideas about wearing sexy lingerie might not have bothered her so much. But as it stood she was feeling like an underdog in her marriage, relatively powerless and dependent. That feeling made her want to back off a little. It also made Chuck's ideas about sex seem degrading. From her perspective it wasn't as if he was just looking for variety and a little sexiness, but that he was reducing her to a sex object.

Can couples like Chuck and Julie, who, after all, have basically good marriages, find their way out of this kind of dilemma? Yes. And as good a place as any to start is with their sex lives.

Egalitarian Sex

Perhaps the simplest way to begin looking at how egalitarian marriages—marriages based on equality—work is to take a look at your own sex life. Take a minute to take this little quiz:

Sex-Role Self-Assessment

As you think back on your sexual relationship, does it seem that *one* of you is mostly responsible for how often you make love? Does each of you feel that you have the right to say no to sex?

When you make love, do you sense that there's some balance in your lovemaking? Overall, do each of you feel that you get as much as you give?

In your opinion, are you and your partner equally concerned with making yourself sexually attractive to the other person? If not, which one of you seems more conscious of trying to be attractive?

Do you and your partner talk much when you make love? Do you feel free to ask your partner to make love to you in a particular way?

Do you feel that it would be okay with your partner if you were to suggest trying something different when you make love? What sort of response would you expect? Have you ever suggested trying something new when you're in bed? Has your partner ever made that kind of suggestion?

In sexual relationships that are egalitarian, one partner does not have all the responsibility for initiating sex. Both partners feel that they have the right to approach the other, and both feel that they have the right to say yes, or no, depending on what they want at the time. Most importantly, in egalitarian sexual relationships partners feel they share *equal* responsibility for making sex fun and fulfilling.

In egalitarian sexual relationships, there is a balance between giving and taking. Sex is a two-way street, and it's equally satisfying to both partners. Each partner is equally motivated to please the other, and each is concerned with being attractive to the other. There is room in these sexual relationships for "special requests," as well as for new ideas. The key is that both partners can ask for what they want, or suggest something new.

Communication and Egalitarian Sex

One characteristic about making love in traditional relationships, where the man is the pursuer and the woman is the object of his passion, is that it doesn't require much in the way of communication. Lovemaking of this kind is basically an enactment of roles, and assuming that both partners pretty much know their parts, communication isn't necessary so much as helpful. Good communication can improve the chances of it being an *arousing* sexual experience. It won't necessarily, however, make it an *intimate* sexual experience. And it won't necessarily keep sexual desire thriving over the years.

Overcoming inhibitions about sexual communication—to free people up so that they're able to let their partners know what turns them on and what doesn't—is basic to sex therapy. Every good sex therapist since Masters and Johnson has helped men and women overcome sexual dysfunctions such as impotence and anorgasmia partly by teaching the basic rules of sexual communication. What are these rules?

The main forms of communication that sex therapists have helped couples develop are *telling* and *showing*. They teach people to tell each other how and where they want to be touched. When talking isn't enough—where it doesn't seem to be working—couples are encouraged to show each other what they want. Basically this involves touching yourself while your partner watches and learns.

Learning to communicate effectively through talking and showing can enhance almost any sexual relationship, up to a point. It can cure a lot of frustrating sexual dysfunctions. And if that's where your sex life happens to be bogged down, it can be very helpful to learn how to show and tell.

As important as it can be, communication on the level of sexual technique—in other words, telling and showing—is only one kind of communication. It's what I call *technical communication*. It's important, since without it sex may not be physically arousing, and may even result in sexual dysfunction.

There is another level of sexual communication, though, that's related to intimacy and sexual desire more than to physical arousal. Without good technical communication, sex may not be physically arousing; but without the other kind of communication, it probably won't be intimate.

This other kind of communication is what I call *emotional communication*. Emotional communication has less to do with the "how-to's" of lovemaking than it does with sharing your state of mind, your feelings. Emotional communication allows lovemaking to go beyond technique and to become a way to achieve intimacy. It moves a sexual relationship beyond the level of an unintimate enactment of roles to the level of an intimate encounter between real people.

221

What's wrong with sex roles, you might ask? Well, they lead to boredom and frustration, for one thing. Talk to women, and they'll tell you how boring the traditional woman's role in sex really is. Being a sex object may be exciting and flattering when you're a teenager, but as a role in life it wears pretty thin after a while. It's not a role that most women find enjoyable for ten or twenty years. After a while, they say, you get more anxious and insecure about how you look. You get tired of having to be indirect about your sexual desires, and more than a little resentful about your partner's sexual laziness.

Traditional sex is no more exciting for men in the long run than it is for women. Men may like to pursue at first, but as times goes by they get more and more bored being the initiator over and over again. Then they start getting lazy about it. They put less and less effort into the game. Whereas in the beginning they may have taken a lot of time getting their partner turned on during foreplay, after a while it gets repetitious, and they start losing their motivation. Sex stops being something spontaneous, and becomes something routine. Foreplay stops being fun and creative, and start becoming repetitious work. The whole sexual encounter gets shorter and shorter, with more interest in getting it over with than on making it last.

As frustrating and unfulfilling as these traditional sexual roles may be, for men and women alike, it isn't necessarily easy to get them to change. Men may be bored with being the initiator, but that doesn't mean they will be receptive to the idea of their partners taking the initiative. Similarly, women may resent the passive role, yet resist the idea of being more active in sex.

Traditional sex is not only boring and frustrating in the long run, but also clearly places women in a one-down position. In terms of power, women have been put in the role of saying yes or no, but not of having the power of initiation. To some extent the sexual revolution changed that, though many women continue to complain that their partners get uncomfortable if they

become aggressive in sex. Here are the telltale signs of this ambivalence:

- As a woman, have you ever had the feeling that your partner would like you to be sexually responsive, but that he
  feels uncomfortable if you "take over" sex too much, or too
  often?
- As a man, have you ever felt uncomfortable with your partner's being too sexually "aggressive"? How would you feel
  if she were the one to initiate sex all the time, and your role
  was simply to say either yes, or no?

Egalitarian sexual relationships are built on emotional communication as much as they're built on good technical communication. What is emotional communication? Think about some
of the different times you've made love over the past year or
two. Chances are, if you count yourself as sexually liberated,
you can look back on these sexual experiences and honestly say
that you are able to let your partner know what you wanted, at
least in a technical sense. In other words, you are probably good
at technical communication in bed. But that's not the same thing
as saying that you were able let your partner know what you
were looking for on an *emotional* level when you made love.

Anyone who takes a minute to think about their sex life over
the past year will quickly realize that they were not always in
the same *mood* when they made love. Sometimes they may have
been happy, sometimes a little sad or lonely. Sometimes they
may have been feeling playful, at other times serious. Sometimes they may have felt like they wanted to be taken care of,
distracted, or entertained. At other times they may have been in
a giving mood. And so on.

It makes sense that people don't always approach sex with
the same emotional "set." After all, we aren't automatons—sexual machines that work the same way, and want the same things,
time after time. We're complex human beings, with moods that
change and that reflect our changing needs. When we can com-

municate those changing moods, and integrate our changing needs into our lovemaking, we find that sex can make us feel intimate. In contrast, when we find that we need to put our moods aside, and keep our emotional needs out of sex, we will discover that making love can be physically arousing but emotionally empty.

Too much emphasis on technical communication, and not enough on emotional communication, is why a lot of people have become turned off to sexual liberation. The media, following on what sex therapists were doing, have played up technical communication to the hilt. The result is that most people feel fed up to the gills with information and advice on sexual how-to's, yet still feel that something is missing from their sex lives. Physically they may be very satisfied from sex, but emotionally it leaves them hungry.

You learn to communicate emotionally by learning to identify and label your own moods. However, if you don't pay attention to how you're feeling, you can't possibly develop any skill at emotional communication. If that's where you (or your partner) are at, you need to do some basic work on paying attention and labeling your feelings. You need to know when you're feeling happy versus sad, lonely versus involved, playful versus serious, and so on.

Once you know what you're feeling, you have an opportunity to bring those feelings into your lovemaking, to have sex be a way of communicating and sharing, as well as a way of feeling good. It's a beautiful thing when making love can make us feel loved, or less lonely, or secure, as well as physically excited.

Intimate lovemaking is lovemaking that's open to emotional *and* technical communication. Intimate lovers let each other know, in one way or another, not just how they want to be touched, but how they're *feeling*. They share their moods and their needs. They know if the other person is feeling playful, or if they're feeling lonely, if they feel happy and carefree, or tense and worried. Sex changes, depending on the emotional states that each partner brings into it. They don't try to exclude their emotions from lovemaking; on the contrary, they try to use lovemaking creatively to meet each other's emotional (as well as physical) needs.

One couple I know, who are good at emotional communication and who also have what feels to them like a very intimate sexual relationship, are very good at letting each other know what they're feeling, both in and out of the bedroom. This helps, because they usually know pretty well where the other person is at *before* they start making love. Though they occasionally have their conflicts, usually they're able to tailor their sexual encounters—*what* they do in bed—to meet both their emotional needs. When one is feeling tense or lonely, for example, there may be a lot of holding and hugging in the early stages of a sexual encounter. When one is feeling playful or naughty, and the other is up for it, there may be more experimentation than usual. Sometimes there's a lot of laughter, sometimes just quiet tenderness. Their sexual encounters are rarely the same from time to time, and they seem in no danger of falling into a rut, much less losing their sexual desire.

Because this couple is able to communicate emotionally does not mean that they don't communicate technically. Technical communication is also there; it's just secondary to emotional communication.

How good are you at *emotional* communication, as opposed to *technical* communication? Do you think you can get in touch with your emotional state from day to day and communicate it to your partner? Would you want to know about your partner's emotional state? What effect do you think good emotional communication would have on your sex life? What effect do you think it might have on how intimate you feel?

Couples who enjoy egalitarian sex lives are less tied to traditional roles in their relationship in general, and in their sexual relationship in particular. In bed they're less constrained by habit and rote repetition. This protects them from boredom. These couples have progressed to the point where their sexual relationship has an identity of its own. It lives and grows right alongside their individual identities. It thrives on sharing and openness. It's flexible and creative. In these relationships, everything from making money to making love is fair game for negotiation and compromise.

The above are some ideas about what you need in order to have an egalitarian *sexual* relationship. Being equals in bed is vital to having a sex life that is mutually satisfying and stays alive over the years. Anything less is pretty much doomed to fail, sooner or later. Why? Because the partner who feels *less equal* is the one who will eventually feel sexually short-changed and will eventually lose interest in it.

Being equals in bed is important to good sex; but being equals out of bed is vital to the intimacy that's the foundation of a good relationship. Let's look at how you can work toward that goal.

Building Egalitarian Relationships

Part 1: Overcoming Lopsidedness

Love and intimacy can deepen and grow only in relationships between equals. Whenever one partner in a relationship begins to feel one-down to the other, that person is going to hold back, be less revealing, less willing to be vulnerable. That will undermine the closeness in the relationship. Just how much holding back goes on depends on just how "unequal" one partner feels to the other. A person who feels powerless will be guarded. Feelings of powerlessness also make a person withdraw sexually. One of the most common causes of lost sexual desire is this feeling of being one-down in a relationship.

On one level relationships that are lopsided in terms of power work to the advantage of the one who has more power. On some issues that person gets their way. In terms of being able to sustain intimacy and sexual desire, though, lopsided relationships don't work. If you want intimacy to grow, and if you want to keep sexual passion alive over the years, you need to establish a relationship between equals. Here are some guidelines for doing that.

Dealing With Power. Probably the best way to make sure that one partner in a relationship is going to end up feeling one-down is to avoid dealing with the issue of power. When one or both of you gets into the habit of avoiding conflicts and arguments, you're doing just that. Then you set the stage for feeling resentful, and for holding back.

The issue of power—basically, of making *decisions*—is really unavoidable in any relationship. If you think you can avoid the issue of power by avoiding arguments or conflicts, you're wrong. Decisions will end up being made, but you may feel that you didn't have a voice in them. Then you'll feel resentful, and sooner or later you'll start closing up and holding back.

In the best of egalitarian relationships the issue of power and control is handled on an ongoing basis. In these relationships decisions are made through a more or less continual process of negotiation and compromise. That's not to say there's constant conflict in these relationships; on the other hand, they aren't conflict-free. As partners mature in an egalitarian relationship, they learn to handle their conflicts more effectively. As they become comfortable and secure as equals, they have less need to resort to techniques like shouting or threatening to try to get their way. They become better at negotiating, and they learn the virtues of compromise.

Individuals who are threatened by the idea of being equals have a hard time compromising. To insecure people a compromise feels like a loss. They'll resort to almost anything to get their way, to avoid having to compromise. Sometimes they succeed, and get what they want through intimidation, guilt, or whatever works. But they end up defeating themselves by causing their partners to close off.

Individuals who were intimidated as children, and who learned to give up rather than fight, will be inclined to do the same in their adult relationships. They may be too easily discouraged from trying to get what they want. By avoiding conflicts and giving in, they buy peace, but at the price of intimacy and sexual desire.

When you run into a couple that has an egalitarian relationship, what strikes you most is the awareness you have of each partner's personality. These people have a real sense of who they are as individuals. You don't have to guess a lot about what they think, or feel, or want; they tend to be pretty upfront about these things. You get the feeling they can handle conflicts, but you don't get the feeling they're bullies. They have what's sometimes referred to as "presence." At the bottom line, it's their persistent willingness to face issues, and to settle conflicts through negotiation and compromise that enables people in these kinds of relationships to grow, together and individually. It's a key to making marriage work.

Money and Equality. Julie, if you'll recall, felt uncomfortable because she'd given up work to stay home with her two children while they were babies. Even though her husband Chuck was not a dominating, controlling type of man, Julie felt uncomfortable being financially dependent on him. She felt vulnerable and depressed. As I talked with her more about these feelings, it became clear that they played a major role in her loss of sexual desire, and in her withdrawal from Chuck. It turned out he'd noticed it, too, but figured it was some kind of reaction to motherhood.

"I noticed," Chuck said, "that Julie became a different person after our first was born. She seemed mild, almost passive in fact. I was used to her spunky personality, but she became quieter, and there was a lot less spark in her. I thought maybe she was just tired, or that motherhood had mellowed her out. Now that we're talking about it, I realize it was probably something else. Also, that was the time she started losing interest in sex."

I asked Julie why she thought that had happened to her.

"I think I'm more aware of it, like Chuck is, now that I can look back on it. At the time I thought I was going through a little postnatal depression, or maybe missing work. It can be lonely being housebound with an infant. But also I remember thinking a couple of times that I was really at a disadvantage because of my financial dependency on Chuck. I remember feeling vulnerable a lot, but never talking about it. I think I felt embarrassed about it. There were one or two occasions I can remember when we argued over something that had to do with money. I distinctly remember giving in, not because I agreed with Chuck, but because on some level I thought I *had* to give in. Because it seemed like *Chuck's* money. It's like I said before, in my mind money has always been equated with power. Deep down I believe that a woman without money is a woman without power. That's the way it was for my mother. She never had an independent income, and she never made any decisions."

Julie's thinking wasn't neurotic or crazy. In this world, money *is* power, and the person without any means of earning money has very little power.

How do you handle money in your relationship? Do you each have a way of earning an independent income? What would life be like, for each of you, without the other person's income?

If you don't have an income of your own, how does that make you feel? Do you feel at a disadvantage when making decisions about spending money? Do you find yourself giving in a lot on those kinds of decisions? Does your partner resent your making suggestions if you're not making the money?

If you don't have an income, think about doing something that would earn you one. The fact is that you may never feel, or be treated, like an equal without it.

Responsibility and Equality. How do you and your partner divide responsibilities for day-to-day living? Who cleans the bath-

room, who does the cooking? Who stops for groceries, and who
vacuums? Who manages the budget, and who pays the bills?

In egalitarian relationships these kinds of responsibilities tend
to get more or less evenly distributed between partners.

Do you do more than your fair share (in other words, more
than half) of the chores? Do you do more of the "dirty" chores?
If so, what's the reason?

In relationships that are unequal, one partner usually gets
more of the "chores" than the other. Usually, it's the one who
has less power who gets more chores to do, or the "dirty" chores.
Somehow, the other person's time is considered more valuable,
too valuable, for instance, to be spent cleaning a bathtub.

To start putting your relationship on a more egalitarian footing, make a list of all the "chores" that have to be done on a
regular basis. Be sure to include things like taking out the
rubbish, emptying the dishwasher, cleaning the toilet, and
washing clothes.

After you've completed your list, go through it, and after each
item, write your name if you almost always do it, your partner's
name if he or she almost always does it, or both your names if
you each do that chore more or less equally often.

How does your list look? Does it seem unbalanced toward one
of you or the other? Which one of you seems to be doing more
of the low-status work in your household? If you wanted to even
things out more, what chores would you each give up or take
on?

Decisions, Decisions. Sharing power means sharing decisions.
That doesn't mean that people in egalitarian relationships make
every single decision together; nor does it mean that they never
do anything as individuals. It does mean, though, that they make
important decisions together.

Nowhere is the difference between the relationship that's basically egalitarian, versus one that isn't, more obvious than when

it comes to the big decisions, especially decisions related to goals, major purchases, and planning.

How are big decisions made in your relationship?

- How do you decide where you'll live?
- Who decides when and where you'll go on holiday?
- Who decides what furniture you'll buy?
- How do you decide on major purchases, like which car or house to buy?
- How do you choose mutual friends, and others you spend a lot of your free time with?

In lopsided relationships the big decisions are made by one person. That person's taste in furniture, or houses, or cars, has a way of prevailing. Where that person likes to holiday is where they holiday. They live where that person wants to live, and they associate with the people who that person wants as friends. There is surprisingly little communication in lopsided relationships.

Egalitarian relationships don't work this way. In egalitarian relationships it isn't always one partner who's making the big decisions. Planning in particular is something that's done through negotiation and compromise. There's a lot of communication in egalitarian relationships.

If it seems that your relationship is lopsided, and that one of you is "more equal" than the other, then one of you needs to learn to be more assertive, while the other needs to learn something about the art of compromise. A good way to start is to begin talking and listening to each other every day. Set aside some time for this, and stick to it. Don't argue or defend yourselves—just listen and talk.

If you find yourself at the bottom of a lopsided relationship, chances are you feel withdrawn, vulnerable, and guarded. That feeling may extend to your sexuality, which may also be more or less closed off. To work your way out of this you need to assert yourself more. Don't expect your partner to simply hand over 50 percent of the power in your relationship. Don't sit there waiting for him or her to include you in major decisions if you haven't played a role in them before. Don't expect plans to include your input if you haven't let your preferences be known. If you want to be an equal, you need to *work* toward being an equal.

Part 2: Overcoming Territoriality

Heather and Gary were having a hard time of it. Through two years of steady dating and another two of living together, things had been just great between them. He'd wanted to get married, but she said she wasn't ready yet. So they went ahead and bought a house together. That's when things started going downhill.

They were both feeling frustrated. Gary felt that Heather had changed dramatically after they'd bought the house. He was beginning to feel sorry that he'd become involved in the first place. I asked him to put his feelings into words. He needed just two: "Squeezed out!"

Heather thought Gary was crazy. From her perspective he was the one with the problem. "I'm not squeezing anyone out," she said. "I'm just watching out for myself."

I turned to Gary again and asked him to explain what he meant.

One of the first things that Gary had noticed about living with Heather was her concern about keeping their possessions separate. In fact, he said, it was a virtual preoccupation on her part. At first he didn't make much of it. He thought it was just a quirk. But looking back on it, he said, it should have told him something. Everything from records to furniture, it seemed, had to be put into one of two categories: *his* or *hers*. Every time she'd buy something, the first thing she'd do was put *her* name on it. When she came home one day with a new vacuum cleaner and proceeded to etch her name into its plastic case, he had a minor fit.

Another thing that Gary noticed—and this bothered him a lot more—was that Heather never wanted to share the cost of anything. Not that she wouldn't pay for anything; she just didn't want to *share* the expense. Whatever it was that they needed, she preferred that one or the other of them buy it. For example, there was the lawnmower. Gary said that if they could each pay half, they could buy a better one than he could afford alone. But Heather turned him down. She said she'd rather that they either not buy it at all, or else wait until one of them could afford it. He went along, but it bothered him.

After they bought the house, Gary found himself getting more and more resentful about the way Heather seemed obsessed with dividing their lives into separate territories. It struck him that she resisted sharing space as much as she resisted sharing possessions. He began to realize that the house itself was divided into *his* rooms and *her* rooms. *His* rooms included the den, the garage, and the cellar; *hers* included the kitchen, the bedrooms, and the living room. He could do pretty much whatever he liked in *his* rooms, but if he even so much as moved a couch pillow, he'd find it back where it started the next time he passed through the living room.

Gary was hurt and confused. He wondered whether he was being unreasonable and oversensitive. Was Heather just being a typical woman, wanting to decorate the house her way? Was he imagining it, or was she really drawing lines all over the place? Was he being squeezed out, or was he being too possessive?

Questions like these are difficult to answer. Every one of us has one side of a story to tell. Heather naturally felt justified in being the way she was. Privately she admitted that maybe sometimes she was overly concerned with the issue of what belonged to whom, and who paid for what. On the other hand, she'd been in relationships with men who took the attitude that everything, including her, was theirs. She'd felt dominated and exploited, and she didn't want it to happen again. She thought that the best insurance against that happening with Gary was to keep the boundaries between them clear, even if that meant hurting his feelings once in a while.

Regardless of whether or not it was justified by past experience, Heather had to face the fact that her territorial behavior was having some negative effects on her relationship. It was having the effect it intended, which was to establish some form of equality between them, but it was also turning their relationship into a corporate one, based on a philosophy of equal but separate, rather than of equal and shared.

The more Gary pushed for common ground, the harder Heather dug her heels in. The harder he tried to break down territorial fences, the sturdier she built them. Eventually, he started to give up and withdraw. He started talking to her less, about fewer things that mattered. Their communication deterioted to the level of small talk, and eventually very little of that. He took up more outside activities, and started working longer hours. He became less affectionate in general, and pursued her sexually less often.

Heather's reaction to Gary's withdrawal was: "I knew it!" She'd gone into the relationship with a lot of distrust, expecting something to go wrong at any time. She had the same negative expectations about all men: that sooner or later they'd let her down. From my perspective, though, I told her it didn't seem that Gary had let her down, so much as she'd created her own self-fulfilling prophecy.

Looking around at your own physical surroundings is a good way to get in touch with how much territoriality might be an issue in your relationship. Start by making a rough schematic drawing of the layout of your house or flat. Don't worry about drawing to scale, or making it pretty; just make sure you include all the rooms in your drawing. Don't fill in any furniture yet. If there is more than one floor in your home, make a separate floor plan for each one.

Now, take a tour of your home, physically or just mentally, and start to fill in your floor plan, room by room. Put in the furniture and the decorations. Spend a few minutes on each room,

getting the "feel" of it. As you do this, try answering the following questions for yourself:

- Does your space seem to be divided into separate territo-
  ries? Do there seem to be areas that are more or less yours,
  and others that are more or less your partner's?
- Are there shared spaces—common ground—as well as personal spaces? How much "feels" like space that belongs to
  both of you, versus space that belongs to one or the other?
- Does it feel like there is enough shared space in your home?
  Would you like more shared space? More personal space?
- Do you have any space of your own?
- Do you and your partner have shared possessions, as well
  as individual ones? Does everything seem divided into
  "mine" and "yours," or are there some things that are
  "ours"?

When they did this exercise, one couple reported that all of
the space in their house, with the exception of a tiny side room
off the den, felt like it was *his* space. Not only wasn't there much
space that was *hers*, but there also wasn't any *shared* space: no
rooms that felt like they were *theirs*. The furniture, for example,
all reflected *his* taste. Each room was decorated with art that *he*
liked. And so on.

The territoriality in this couple's house mirrored their relationship as a whole. Most everything they owned was in his
name. Their bank account was in his name. When they went
out to eat, it was to a restaurant that he chose, and it was paid
for using his credit cards. And so on. Early on in the relationship
this arrangement was satisfactory to both of them, but as the
years went by the wife felt more and more unhappy with it.
Naturally, her husband wasn't thrilled when he found his wife's
once-accepting attitude changing. While he was right—that it
was she who was trying to change the rules—he also had to
realize that it was his territorial behavior as much as his wife's
need for recognition that was straining their marriage. She just

couldn't feel close to or sexually interested in him as long as he refused to share power and be an equal. The harder he held on to everything, and the more he resisted sharing, the more he locked intimacy, sexual passion, and love out of his marriage.

Relationships that are suffering from the effects of territoriality are relationships where trust and self-esteem are issues— sometimes hidden issues—for one or both partners. They are hidden issues in the sense that being territorial usually covers up distrust, or compensates for low self-esteem. This was true for both of the couples described above. Being territorial gave the territorial person a sense of control that helped make up for their inability to trust. Both of them were holding back from their partners, refusing to relate to them as equals, and their partners held back in return. In both relationships love was slowly dying, and though they were committed, that commitment alone would probably not be enough to sustain these couples for the rest of their lives.

Trust and self-esteem were the subjects of Part IV, and by now you may have started working on those areas. But you can also work together, right now, on this issue of territoriality and shared space. Your goal is to achieve some *balance* in your relationship between shared space and personal space. There's nothing wrong with wanting some personal space; in other words, with having some separate territories. On the other hand, you also need some common ground. This common ground forms the basis for intimacy and nourishes sexual desire.

Learning to share may mean learning to give up some control, or learning to be more assertive. It may not be very comfortable at first. It can arouse anxiety. Indeed, building a common ground can lead to conflicts that need to be ironed out through negotiation. As difficult as this may sound, you might actually find yourselves feeling closer, and even more passionate about each other, too, at the same time that you confront and work through issues that have separated you.

❦   ❦   ❦

The notion of territoriality, and how it can affect your relationship, can be extended to any area of your life. It doesn't have to be limited to your physical space. That was only one example of it. You can apply this same concept, and this same technique, to other parts of your relationship; for example, to money, recreation, or friendships. The more areas you find that seem to be divided up into separate territories—into *yours* and *mine*—the more likely it is that you either have a *lopsided* relationship, where one of you is calling all the shots, or a *corporate* relationship based on the separate-but-equal idea. What you need is an *egalitarian* relationship, where equality is achieved through compromise and the creation of common ground.

Egalitarian Relationships Versus Corporate Relationships

The essence of an egalitarian marriage is sharing, and the key to it is negotiation. Egalitarian relationships have a feeling of equality about them, but it's a particular kind of equality, one that's rooted in confrontation instead of avoidance, and which is based more on compromise than on territoriality. There's a lot of negotiation that goes on (and on, and on!) in this kind of relationship. There's a great deal of mutual involvement in decisions and plans. Obviously, all this negotiating and compromising means that there's a lot of communication. Partners in egalitarian relationships talk to each other a lot. They confront a lot of issues and reach a lot of compromises through talking and listening to each other.

There's another kind of relationship, which is also based on equality in a way, but that isn't what I mean by egalitarian. That's the *corporate* relationship. In a corporate relationship, partners achieve equality by *not* sharing, by *not* becoming too involved, and by *not* communicating. To see if you may be in this kind of relationship, answer these questions:

- Do you and your partner have any common savings accounts, or are all your accounts separate?
- Do you and your partner ever rotate chores, so that each of you takes turns, or does each of you always take care of your own separate set of responsibilities?
- Do you feel the need to discuss major purchases you make before you make them, or do you feel free to buy what you want as long as it's your own money you're spending?
- Do you pay bills out of a joint bank account, or do you each pay separate bills out of individual accounts?
- Do you decide together what kind of cars or furniture you're going to get, or does each of you buy what you individually like?

In corporate relationships, equality is based on territoriality, and is achieved through separation. Partners in a corporate relationship have separate responsibilities, separate finances, separate possessions, and in many ways make separate decisions and lead separate lives. Some people think that's liberated.

Corporate relationships are cool and detached. There isn't much arguing, because very little is decided together. In this kind of relationship, I have my responsibilities and you have yours. I can get angry if you don't live up to your part of the "contract," but I don't feel obligated to do your work for you. I have my own money, which I don't have to account to you for, and you have yours. So long as I can pay my share of the bills, I feel free to buy whatever I want with "my" money. You have no say-so about whether I spend my money on a Porsche, or give it away to charity. I don't feel beholden to you, and I'm not financially dependent on you. I have my own career, and you have yours. I have my own hobbies, and probably my own friends, just like you have yours.

Can corporate marriages work? Yes. But they're not very intimate. In corporate relationships partners can feel equal. They can feel freed from dependency and domination, but they may not feel very close or connected. These relationships may last, but they aren't likely to be very passionate. They may be committed, but I wonder how much they're in love.

Egalitarian relationships represent true liberation. As far as relationships go, they're the promised land. Corporate relationships represent a halfway point, a resting place somewhere between traditional relationships, which are so often lopsided, and egalitarian relationships, the kind we need to build.

Those couples who have moved beyond traditional roles, and who have achieved an equality that goes beyond a corporate arrangement, can tell you that egalitarianism opens the door to satisfactions they'd never known. It opens relationships to a deepening and growing intimacy. It enables partners to develop more of their potentials than they'd ever dreamed was possible.

The intimacy that grows (and grows) in an egalitarian relationship creates a bond unlike any other. Couples in egalitarian relationships are obviously passionate about each other, and it's obvious why. In striking out for equality, they've struck real gold. The playfulness, the sensitivity, and the mutual interest in this kind of a relationship is impressive to behold. And it's possible for *you* to have it.

Index

Abusive relationships, 149–51, 208
  child abuse, 192–93, 201, 203
Acceptance, and intimacy, 39–41
Achievement, and self-esteem, 172
Action, 13–14
Affection, withdrawal of, 89
Age, and sexuality, 56–60
Aggression, passive, 113–14, 115
Alienation, 5, 12, ff.
  fear of, 64
Ambivalent attitudes, 110–15
Anger, 87–92, 126–27
Appearance, 61, 139–42, 159–61
Assertiveness, 186–89, 231–32
Attitudes, change of, 209–12
Avoidance, 169
  of conflict, 98–100

Betrayal, sense of, 203, 208, 209
Body image, 29–32, 143–61
  and abuse in childhood, 193
Bulimia, 143

Carpenter, Edward, 52, 165
Careers, and relationships, 78
Change, 105–10, 209–12
Child abuse, 192–93, 201, 203, 204
Children, self-esteem of, 173
Climacteric, 58, 59–60
Clothes, 160
Commitment, 4
  to love, 105
  and priorities, 101–5
Communication, 15–16, 68, 91, ff.
  assertive, 186–89
  and egalitarian sex, 220–26
Conflict, 91, 98–101
  avoidance of, 19, 87, 133–34
Confrontation, 43, 91, ff.
  avoidance of, 17, 19, 133–34
  and power issues, 43
Cooperative approaches to intimacy,
  93–115
Corporate relationships, 94–98, 234,
  237–39

Decisions, 227, 230–31, 238
Denial, 113
Diet, 158–59
Distrust, 19, 193–211. *See also* Trust.
Distrustful people, 48–49
Dominant partners, 25
 and low self-esteem, 23–24

Eating disorders, 143
Emotional blocks, 81–87
Emotional communication, 221, 223–25
Emotional uses of sex, 8
Emotional wounds, healing of, 154–55, 205–8
Emotions, resistance to, 132, 134
Encouragement of change, 109–10
Equality in relationships, 115, 163–64, 213, 220, 226–39
 and intimacy, 39–43, 67–68
 and self-esteem, 46–47
Erotic stimuli, 122
 literature, 139
 writing, 138
Exercise, physical, 158–59
Exercises in relationship, 72–76
Expectations, 115
Expression, problems of, 15–16, 84.
 See also Communication.

Family background. *See also* Personal history.
 and avoidance of conflict, 99
 and distrust, 201–2
 and priorities, 103–4
 and relationships, 95, 106–8
 and self-esteem, 19, 169–70, 172–76
Fears of intimacy, 14–20, 62–67
Fighting, rules for, 100–101
Financial dependence, 215, 218–19, 228–29
 in corporate relationships, 238
Fromm, Erich, 62

Gender-role conflict, 32–34

Grooming, 160–61
 and sexuality, 141–42

Hidden ambivalences, 110–15
Holding back, 14–20, 168
 emotional blocks, 85, 86
 and sense of powerlessness, 22
Hormonal changes of aging, 60
Hormones, and sexuality, 120
Hysterectomy, 36

Identity problems, and self-esteem, 46
Illness, and sexuality, 145–49
Individual approaches to intimacy, 69–92
Individuality, 94
 in egalitarian relationships, 228
 and intimacy, 65
Insight, 13–14
Intimacy, 4, 9–13, 20, ff.
 commitment to, 105
 fear of, 14–20, 62–67
 and gender-role conflict, 32
 and self-esteem, 44, 165–171
 and sexual desire, 60–61, 104
 and territoriality, 236
 and trust, 47, 49, 192–93, 202–3, 210

Journal, sexual-fantasy, 135–37

Kinsey, Alfred, 57

Limits, setting of, 178–83
Loneliness, 166
Love, 5–6, 71, ff.
 commitment to, 105
 falling out of, 12–20, 74, 114
 and sex, 8
 and trust, 203, 210
Loves Coming of Age (Carpenter), 52

Malaise, 12
Male climacteric, 58, 59–60

Manipulative use of emotions, 86, 89
Media, and body images, 152
Men, emotional blocks, 82
Menopause, 58–59
Money, and equality in relationships, 228–29. *See also* Financial dependence.
Monogamy, 4

Negative assertiveness, 187
Negotiation, 68, 101, 115, 170–71, 237
    in egalitarian relationships, 227, 228
Nutrition, 158–59

Open ambivalence, 111

Partners, sex problems of, 35–38
Passive aggression, 113–14, 115
Perls, Frederick, 62
Personal space, 104–5
    priorities, 103
    and relationships, 94–95
Positive assertiveness, 187
Power issues, 25
    and anger, 89
    and equality in relationships, 227–28
    and intimacy, 39–43, 65–68
    in sex roles, 222–23
Powerlessness, sense of, 17, 19, 22–26, 41
    and anger, 88
    and loss of sexual desire, 226
Psychological abuse, 204

Rejection, 89
    and self-esteem, 26–27
Responsibility, in corporate relationships, 238
Romantic love, 163

Self-esteem, 43–47, 164, 165–89
    and abuse in childhood, 193
    and body image, 29–32, 144–45
    and emotional blocks, 86
    and intimacy, 17, 19, 66, 191–92
    low, 22–24

and physical appearance, 159–61
and power issues, 25
and territoriality, 236
Sex, 7–8, 219–37
Sex roles, 34, 222
    self-assessment, 219–20
Sex therapy, 4–6, 221
Sexual blocks, 85–87, 121
Sexual desire, 12, 20, 119–22
    and body image, 31–32
    and equality in relationships, 227
    and gender-role conflict, 32
    and intimacy, 60–61, 104, 166
    lack of, 21–38
    loss of, 88
    problems of, 5–6, 9–13, 18
    and self-esteem, 44, 166, 168–71
    and trust, 202–3
Sexual fantasies, 27–29, 119, 123, 128–32
    techniques, 135–39
Sexual interest history, 72–74
Sexuality, 61
    and age, 56–60
    and gender-role conflict, 33
    repression of, 86–87
    resistance to, 123–27
    and trust, 192–93
Shared space, 103–5
Sharing, 236–37
    and trust, 208
Stress, 76–81
Surgery, and sexuality, 145–49

Technical communication, 221, 224
Territoriality, 232–37
    in corporate relationships, 238
Testosterone, 60, 120
Therapy, 4–6, 155, 208, 221
Touching, problems of, 35
Traditional sex roles, 220, 222–23
Trust, 47–52, 164, 191–211
    and intimacy, 66
    and territoriality, 236
Trustful people, 200–201

Understanding, 13–14
Unresolved conflict, 74, 96

Vulnerability:
  and emotional blocks, 81–82
  and intimacy, 49

Walls of anger, 87–92, 126–27
Weight control, 143
Widowhood, and sexual activity, 57–58
Withdrawal, and hidden ambivalence, 113